THE FAMILIAR STRANGER

(RE)INTRODUCING THE HOLY SPIRIT TO THOSE IN SEARCH OF AN EXPERIENTIAL SPIRITUALITY

BIBLE STUDY GUIDE | SIX SESSIONS

TYLER STATON

HarperChristian Resources

The Familiar Stranger Bible Study Guide
Copyright © 2026 by Tyler Staton

Published by HarperChristian Resources, 3950 Sparks Drive SE, Suite 101, Grand Rapids, MI 49546, USA. Harper-Christian Resources is a registered trademark of HarperCollins Christian Publishing, Inc.

Requests for information should be addressed to customercare@harpercollins.com.

ISBN 978-0-310-18268-9 (softcover)
ISBN 978-0-310-18269-6 (ebook)

HarperChristian Resources titles may be purchased in bulk for church, business, fundraising, or ministry use. For information, please e-mail ResourceSpecialist@ChurchSource.com.

HarperCollins Publishers, Macken House, 39/40 Mayor Street Upper, Dublin 1, D01 C9W8, Ireland (https://www.harpercollins.com).

Art direction: Ron Huizinga
Cover Design: © 2025 HarperCollins Christian Publishing
Interior Design: Rob Williams / InsideOut Design

First Printing December 2025 / Printed in the United States of America

CONTENTS

A NOTE FROM TYLER

There's a moment near the end of Jesus' ministry when he pulls Peter, James, and John in close enough to get a glimpse of his glory. He leaves the other nine behind and takes these three on a hike up Mount Tabor, and it's there at the summit that he begins to glow with heavenly splendor. Moses and Elijah, both remembered for face-to-face encounters with God on mountaintop summits, appear alongside Jesus. The voice of God the Father thunders audibly, *"This is my Son, whom I love; with him I am well pleased. Listen to him!"* (Matthew 17:5).

Today, we know this transcendent biblical moment as Christ's "transfiguration," but before we gave it a title, it was just a moment, a spiritual experience that left its witnesses staggering back downhill in awestruck wonder.

Nearly every follower of Jesus whom I know can relate to this moment. Most of us have a "mountaintop experience" or two under our belts, and the way we describe and relate to these moments are as diverse as those on the pages of Scripture. Peter suggested pitching a tent and living forever on the mountaintop. Elijah, encountering God on this very mountain centuries prior, pulled his cloak over his face in reverent fear. Moses went back to the people with renewed zeal, instruction, and a tint of God's glorious glow gleaming on his own common cheeks.

Some of us dismiss these mountaintop moments as trivial, even childish, experiences but not the substance of faith on which to build a life of discipleship.

Others sensationalize such experiences, assuming the extraordinary to be common, trying to drum up a spiritual life under a tent on the mountaintop.

Still others imagine their experience with God inferior if their encounter is deemed less spectacular than the account of another.

These subtle divisions are no more obvious than the litany of ways modern-day Christians describe and relate to the Holy Spirit and his gifts. *The Familiar Stranger* is a book and curriculum written not to assuage believers to adopt a solitary position, gravitating to one perspective or another, but a humble, sincere attempt to invite streams to flow together into a single river. The Holy Spirit, and the experiences often associated with his presence and power both on the pages of the Bible and in our lives today, should not be feared, divisive, or demeaning but the opposite. The Holy Spirit was given so that you'd know the God of love is with you always, even within you.

May the study you are embarking on be one of wading deeper and deeper into God's love until you are swimming in his presence and power through the gift of the Holy Spirit.

— TYLER STATON

HOW TO USE THIS GUIDE

The familiar stranger. For many Christians, that is what the Holy Spirit represents. He is *familiar* in the sense they have heard references to him in podcasts or sermons and read stories about him in the Bible. Stories like the one in Acts 2, where he enters the room like a violent wind, and then what look like tongues of fire rest on each of the believers gathered there, and then they begin speaking in other languages.

Yet it is exactly stories like these that lead many Christians to also view the Holy Spirit as a *stranger.* Why did he enter the room like a violent wind? Why settle on the believers like tongues of fire? Why did he enable them to speak in tongues? Does he still move like this today? Many Christians, even if they are intrigued by the Holy Spirit and want to experience his presence and power, just don't know where to start.

Whether you are thirsty about the Holy Spirit, or suspicious about him, or perhaps uninformed about him, the goal of this study is to meet you where you are, (re)introduce you to the *person* of the Holy Spirit, and then invite you to live clothed in the *power* of the Holy Spirit. Before you begin, know there are a few ways you can go through this material. You can experience this study with others in a group (such as a Bible study, Sunday school class, or other gathering), or you can go through the content on your own. Either way, the videos are available to view at any time by following the instructions provided with this study guide.

GROUP STUDY

Each of the sessions in this study is divided into two parts: (1) a group study section and (2) a personal study section. The group study section provides a basic framework on how to open your time together, get the most out of the video content, and discuss the key ideas that were presented in the teaching. Each session includes the following:

- **Welcome:** A short opening note about the topic of the session for you to read on your own before you meet as a group.

- **Connect:** A few icebreaker questions to get you and your group members thinking about the topic and interacting with each other.
- **Watch:** An outline of the key points covered in each video teaching along with space for you to take notes as you watch each session.
- **Discuss:** Questions to help you and your group reflect on the teaching material presented and apply it to your lives.
- **Respond:** A short personal exercise to help reinforce the key ideas.
- **Pray:** A brief set of prompts to help you and your group take the next step in inviting the Holy Spirit to be present and active in your lives.

If you are doing this study in a group, make sure you have your own copy of the study guide so you can write down your thoughts, responses, and reflections in the space provided—and so you have access to the videos via streaming. You will also want to have a copy of *The Familiar Stranger* book, as reading it alongside this guide will provide you with deeper insights. (See the notes at the beginning of each group session and personal study section on which chapters of the book you should read before the next group session.)

Finally, keep these points in mind:

- **Facilitation:** If you are doing this study in a group, you will want to appoint someone to serve as a facilitator. This person will be responsible for starting the video and keeping track of time during discussions and activities. If *you* have been chosen for this role, there are some resources in the back of this guide that can help you lead your group through the study.

- **Faithfulness:** Your group is a place where tremendous growth can happen as you reflect on the Bible, ask questions, and learn what God is doing in other people's lives. For this reason, be fully committed and attend each session so you can build trust and rapport with the other members.

- **Friendship:** The goal of any small group is to serve as a place where people can share, learn about God, and build friendships. So seek to make your group a safe place. Be honest about your thoughts and feelings, but also listen carefully to everyone else's thoughts, feelings, and opinions. Keep anything personal that your group members share in confidence so that you can create a community where people can heal, be challenged, and grow spiritually.

If you are going through this study on your own, read the opening Welcome section and reflect on the questions in the Connect section. Watch the video and use the outline provided to help you take notes. Finally, personalize the questions and exercises in the Discuss and Respond sections. Close by recording any requests you want to pray about during the week.

PERSONAL STUDY

The personal study is for you to work through on your own during the week. Each exercise is designed to help you explore the key ideas you uncovered during your group time and delve into passages from the Bible that will help you apply those principles. Go at your own pace, doing a little each day—or tackle the material all at once. Remember to spend a few moments in silence to listen to whatever the Holy Spirit might be speaking to you.

If you are doing this study as part of a group and you are unable to finish (or even start) these personal studies for the week, you should still attend the group time. Be assured you are still wanted and welcome even if you don't have your "homework" done. The personal studies are simply intended to help you better hear from the Holy Spirit and learn how to apply what he is saying to your life. So, as you go through this study, be watching for the ways he will guide you in how to lead a Spirit-empowered life in your everyday world.

WEEK 1

BEFORE GROUP MEETING	Read the introduction and chapter 1 in *The Familiar Stranger* Read the Welcome section (page 2)
GROUP MEETING	Discuss the Connect questions Watch the video teaching for session 1 Discuss the questions that follow as a group Do the closing exercise and pray (pages 2–6)
STUDY 1	Complete the personal study (pages 8–10)
STUDY 2	Complete the personal study (pages 11–13)
STUDY 3	Complete the personal study (pages 14–16)
CATCH UP AND READ AHEAD (BEFORE WEEK 2 GROUP MEETING)	Connect with someone in your group Read chapters 2–4 in *The Familiar Stranger* Complete any unfinished personal studies (page 17)

THE FAMILIAR STRANGER

"It is the lived conviction that everything, absolutely everything, in the scriptures is livable. Not just true, but livable. . . . This is the supernatural core, a lived resurrection and Holy Spirit core, of the Christian life."

EUGENE PETERSON, *THE PASTOR: A MEMOIR*[1]

WELCOME | READ ON YOUR OWN

The Bible presents the picture of a *triune* God. He is one God in three persons—a God in communion: Father, Son, and Holy Spirit. We generally comprehend the Father. He is the one "in heaven" (Matthew 6:9) who parents us—"his children" (1 John 3:1 NCV). We know the Son. Jesus came and lived among us, sharing our human experience. He is "not ashamed to call [us] brothers and sisters" (Hebrews 2:11).

The Holy Spirit, though, can seem vague and mysterious—like the third member of a famous band we see in the shadows behind the two lead singers. He is kind of familiar but also the one we don't know all that much about. In fact, a recent survey showed that 60 percent of committed Christians believe the Holy Spirit, the third *person* of the Trinity, is a force to be wielded, not a person to know and be known by.[2] It must break the heart of Jesus that the same Spirit he was so eager to give to his disciples (see John 14:15) has become unknown, feared, and divisive in the church. We are in desperate need of a (re)introduction to the person of the Holy Spirit!

This is the goal of this first session. We will begin by looking at the two ends of the spectrum in which people tend to relate to the Spirit: (1) those who seek his power more than his person on the one side, and (2) those who hold a high view of God's Word but make little of the Spirit's work in their lives on the other. We will then look at what it means for us to engage with the Holy Spirit in *concert* with God's Word . . . for that is what we are after.

Acknowledging where we are when it comes to the Spirit and how we may have mis-learned about (or never known) him is an important first step for all who are hungry for a rich, experiential spirituality. So that is where we'll begin.

CONNECT | 10 MINUTES

If you or any of your group members don't know each other, take a few minutes to introduce yourselves. Then discuss one or both of the following questions:

- Why did you decide to join this study? What do you hope to learn?

  — *or* —

- On a scale of 1 (low) to 5 (high), what is your current level of engagement or experience with the Holy Spirit? Explain your response.

WATCH | 25 MINUTES

Watch the video for this session, which you can access through streaming (see the instructions provided with this guide). Below is an outline of the key points covered during the teaching. Record any key concepts that stand out to you.

OUTLINE

I. **The Triune God: Father, Son, and Spirit**
   A. The Father is God in heaven, parenting all of us, his children.
   B. The Son is Jesus, who came and lived among us, sharing our human experience.
   C. The Spirit is the Holy Spirit, who is present and active from Genesis to Revelation.

II. **The Holy Spirit: Unknown and Misunderstood**
   A. For many of us, the Holy Spirit has become the "familiar stranger."
   B. We are unaware of how he has come and how entirely he has given himself to us.
   C. A troubling gap exists between biblical promises and our modern spiritual experiences.

III. **Jesus' Promise of the Spirit's Presence**
   A. Jesus emphasized the Spirit as better than his physical presence with his disciples.
   B. The Spirit, called Paraclete, offers guidance, comfort, and empowerment.
   C. The disciples struggled to accept the Spirit's role, preferring Jesus' physical presence.

IV. **Challenges in Embracing the Spirit**
   A. The first disciples didn't buy Jesus' vision—and modern disciples don't generally buy it either.
   B. The Spirit is often feared or ignored, which creates division within the church.
   C. Word and Spirit have been pitted against each other in recent church history.

V. **Steps Toward a Spirit-Filled Life**
   A. Rediscover the way of discipleship to Jesus through formative practice and supernatural power.
   B. Pursue a deeper relationship with God through the Spirit's guidance and presence.
   C. Embrace both Word and Spirit for spiritual growth and unity in faith.

NOTES

DISCUSS | 35 MINUTES

Discuss what you just watched by answering the following questions.

1. What does the term "familiar stranger" mean to you when applied to the Holy Spirit? How can the Spirit be both familiar and yet a stranger to believers?

2. In the Gospel of John, the name Jesus gives to the Holy Spirit on several occasions is the Greek *parakletos*. How does your Bible translate this title in John 14:26? What does the term reveal to you about the purpose of the Holy Spirit in our lives?

3. Ask someone to read aloud John 15:26–27. Jesus reveals that we and the Spirit have a similar task. What is it—and why do you think it is so important?

4. Some churches and communities "sensationalize" the Spirit, seeking his power over his person. Others take a high view of knowing God's Word but experience very little of him. Which most resembles your current reality? Explain.

5. Luke begins Acts with this statement: "I wrote about all that Jesus began to do and to teach until the day he was taken up to heaven" (1:1–2). Jesus often gave people an *experience* of God first and then *explained* that experience. Why do you think he did this? What does this reveal about how real transformation happens in our lives?

RESPOND | 10 MINUTES

Take a few minutes to put yourself in the sandals of the disciples as you read through the following passage. Imagine what it would have been like to hear Jesus tell you of his coming departure. These men had risked everything to follow Christ, and now he was going somewhere they could not. This was such a massive disruption that what he said next about the Holy Spirit could have felt like a further letdown—or perhaps a consolation prize. Circle anything in this passage that stands out to you, and then answer the questions that follow.

> "I have told you this, so that when their time comes you will remember that I warned you about them. I did not tell you this from the beginning because I was with you, but now I am going to him who sent me. None of you asks me, 'Where are you going?' Rather, you are filled with grief because I have said these things. But very truly I tell you, it is for your good that I am going away. Unless I go away, the Advocate will not come to you; but if I go, I will send him to you."
>
> JOHN 16:4–7

Notice that Jesus says the disciples didn't ask him where he was going. How can your emotions and feelings cloud you from seeing what Jesus is doing—and how it is actually for your good?

Do you agree with Jesus that the indwelling presence of the Holy Spirit is better than the human presence of Jesus? Or would you trade your current experiences with the Holy Spirit for a face-to-face chat with Jesus? Explain your thoughts.

PRAY | 10 MINUTES

Take a moment as you close to express your deep hunger for a more experiential spirituality. Be honest about your past beliefs about the Holy Spirit, including any limitations, fears, or even lack of interest you have had toward him. Ask God to help you (re)encounter the beauty, truth, and intimacy of the Holy Spirit. Pray to be aware of the Holy Spirit's empowering, transformative, indwelling presence in fresh ways as you begin this study.

PERSONAL STUDY

Oxford scholar Simon Ponsonby emphasized the importance of "experience" when it comes to the Christian faith, stating, "A nonexperiential religion is suspect, for it fails to deal with the totality of our being."[3] Many hunger for this kind of experiential spirituality, but most miss the role the Holy Spirit plays in the process. With this in mind, the personal study portion of this guide is designed to take you deeper into the nature, power, and purpose of the Holy Spirit. The goal here isn't just to acquire more information but to become more fully alive spiritually. After each reading, look up the scriptures provided and write down your responses to the questions. For those engaging in this study as part of a group, you will be given a few minutes to share your insights at the start of the next session. If you are reading *The Familiar Stranger* alongside this study, first review the introduction and chapter 1 in the book.

STUDY 1

WHAT'S MOST MISSING

Billy Graham was one of the world's most respected evangelists. During his lifetime, he preached the gospel to nearly 215 million people in more than 185 countries and territories around the globe. And while every place he went was unique, he noticed a common denominator with those he met: "The desperate need of the nation today is that men and women who profess Jesus be filled with the Holy Spirit."[4] This sense of emptiness was a common global problem—and Billy Graham concluded that what was most missing was the Holy Spirit.

It would have been wonderful if, after announcing what was wrong, believers in Christ took steps to address it. But unfortunately, we have the same desperate need today and, sadly, the Holy Spirit still remains mostly unknown. Yes, Christians *know* about the Holy Spirit. But knowing *about* something and *actually* knowing it are radically different. This is true with people, love, sports, hobbies, and pretty much anything else. Take surfing, for example. You can factually know *about* surfing—the best surfboards, what beaches to visit, how to catch a big wave—but you won't *really* know surfing until you dive into the ocean.

This is why experiential spirituality is such an essential part of faith. It's an approach that helps you know the Bible not merely as ancient teachings and stories but as a lived experience. In the words of David, you can "taste and see that the Lord is good" (Psalm 34:8)—that is, you can experientially know God through your senses. And what about your ongoing hunger for spiritual fulfillment? You satisfy that by being filled with the Holy Spirit (see Acts 4:31).

Experiential spirituality is "what's most missing" in most Christians' faith today. Yet it doesn't have to be! The same Spirit of God that was active at the start of creation (see Genesis 1:2) is available to fill you and help you as a new creation in Christ (see 2 Corinthians 5:17). So, are you ready to receive afresh the gift of God's empowering, uniting, transforming presence?

Read: Psalm 34:8-9; Acts 4:31; Genesis 1:1-2

1. How do you respond to Billy Graham's conclusion about what is "most missing" in the lives of God's people? Do you agree or disagree? Explain your response.

2. According to Acts 4:31, what is one of the traits of being filled with the Spirit? Is that something you are currently experiencing in your life?

> The Holy Spirit is not a New Age, mystical teaching introduced after Jesus. The Spirit was present at creation, named in the Bible's opening lines. In Hebrew, the original language of Genesis, we read, "And the *ruakh* of God was hovering over the waters." The Hebrew *ruakh*, like its Greek counterpart *pneuma*, can be translated into English as either "spirit" or "breath."[5] Later in Genesis we come to this passage: "Then the LORD God formed a man from the dust of the ground and breathed into his nostrils the breath of life, and the man became a living being" (2:7). Genesis often uses the phrase "the breath of life" to describe living creatures (2:7, 6:17). We only have life because God breathes life into us. The same Spirit (or breath) of God that orders and fills all of creation in Genesis 1 fills people with his divine life—and Spirit.[6]

3. Did you realize the Holy Spirit was actively involved in creation (see Genesis 1:2)? What do you think the Spirit was doing within the empty chaos?

4. In Psalm 34:8, David invites us to "taste and see that the LORD is good." What current situation do you need to move from a factual knowledge about God's goodness to actually "tasting" or experiencing his goodness?

The Holy Spirit makes the impractical practice-able. This is what the gifts of the Holy Spirit are all about: making the totally impractical (the supernatural, the miraculous, the gospel ministry of Jesus) not only possible (in extreme situations by super-spiritual people) but practice-able (by ordinary people tabernacled by an extraordinary God). . . . Many believers look at their lives with the honest, sober admission, "If this life, the one I'm experiencing right now, is every-thing the resurrection made possible, I'm underwhelmed." There is a troubling gap between biblical promise and the actual life of the modern disciple. People flock in and out of churches, ordering their lives around the teachings of Jesus, building on the foundation of the Father's love, but totally unaware of how close this triune God has come, how entirely he has given himself to us.[7]

---

5. To what degree do you know the Holy Spirit through actual experiences rather than just what you've read or been taught about him?

O——O——O——O——O——O——O——O——O——O
1   2   3   4   5   6   7   8   9   10

[know about the Holy Spirit]   [experientially know the Holy Spirit]

Based on your rating above, describe an experience you've had with the Holy Spirit—or, if you haven't had any yet, your desire for such an experience.

STUDY 2

FEARFUL BYSTANDERS

It's impossible to describe the rush of a roller coaster to someone who hasn't experienced it firsthand. From a purely logical standpoint, it makes little sense. Why would you get on a giant contraption of metal or wood that goes at breakneck speeds, twists and turns, goes upside down, and drops you at insane angles from incredible heights? Especially on rides with names like "Steel Vengeance," "Skyrush," "Velocicoaster," and "Intimidator 305"?

If you demand to know, control, and have a guarantee about every detail of a roller coaster before trying it, you will likely forever remain a fearful bystander. You will be confused as you witness the very people screaming when they're hundreds of feet up in the air exit the coaster laughing and wanting to ride it again. It won't make any sense to you until you press through your fear and experience it for yourself.

There are a lot of similarities when it comes to how Christians often view the Holy Spirit. Many tend to be suspicious of experience and enamored with explanation: "Teach me everything first, and then maybe I'll be open to the experience." But it's not possible to know everything about the Holy Spirit from a distance. Trying to do that resembles the roller-coaster skeptic stuck in fear while others are experiencing joy.

For this reason, it's important to consider whether there are any past or current beliefs, teachings, or experiences that are filling you with fear about the third person of the Trinity. The Bible assures you that God will take away your fears: "I sought the LORD, and he answered me; he delivered me from all my fears" (Psalm 34:4).

Yet God doesn't just want to take away your fear. He wants to replace it with joy, peace, and hope! Paul describes it this way: "May the God of hope fill you with all joy and peace as you trust in him, so that you may overflow with hope by the power of the Holy Spirit" (Romans 15:13). So don't let fear keep you on the sidelines. The Holy Spirit's power in your life is not to be missed. It is an experience that overflows with hope—not fear.

Read: Psalm 27:1–3; John 9:1–12, 35–41; Romans 15:13

1. What is something that you were initially afraid of doing but then embraced—like going on a roller coaster or bungee jumping? What initial fears did you have to push through?

2. Read Psalm 27:1–3 out loud. Have you made a declaration about your fears in this way? If you have, what was the result?

> Jesus frequently gave people an experience of God first, then explained that experience second. Some tend to be suspicious of experience and enamored with explanation. "Teach me everything first, and then maybe I'll be open to the experience." It's worth remembering that the biblical story is made up of Holy Spirit-saturated, historic accounts of ordinary people experiencing God in various ways, and then, on the other side of that experience, discovering roots for their experience in the unfolding revelation of Yahweh to and through his people.[8]

3. In the story told in John 9:1–12, what "experience of God" did Jesus give the disciples in response to their question? How did Jesus use this miracle in verses 35–41 to then offer spiritual truths to the Pharisees? What is important about the order in this story?

4. What is Paul's prayer that God will "fill you with" in Romans 15:13? What role does the Holy Spirit play in giving you those traits—and what else does Paul say he provides?

Many are led to experience by hunger and curiosity, but at least as many—maybe more—by honest, holy discontent. Clinical psychiatrist Curt Thompson writes, "Despite the interest in spirituality in much of the West, and North America in particular, our overall experience of God's power and life-giving vitality is often limited. We often see life in Jesus as being more about survival than about grace, adventure, and genuine, concrete, life-giving change."[9] A life deeply rooted in Scripture is absolutely essential for a healthy relationship to God, self, others, and the world at large. Equally essential, though, is a life deeply rooted in the Holy Spirit, who leads by experience and functions in partnership, not competition, with the explanatory Holy Bible.[10]

---

5. "Our overall experience of God's power and life-giving vitality is often limited." When it comes to your life in Jesus, which three of the following words do you feel most accurately describe the ways you experience him?

Survival   Grace   Correction   Adventure   Fear   Joy   Rescue   Friendship

Why do these three words most reflect your experiences with Jesus? Are there other words you wish were true for you? If so, what are they?

STUDY 3

THE BOTH/AND KINGDOM

For most things in life, we have to make a choice. Should we fly business class or coach? Get ice cream or frozen yogurt? Buy or rent? So much of our culture is based on an either/or filter. And sometimes, neither option seems great. Over time, we can start to believe God's kingdom operates the same way. The result is that we end up needlessly debating our stance on questions such as: Does our church embrace the Bible *or* the Holy Spirit? Is a contemplative *or* a charismatic experience more spiritual? Does our small group embrace the gospel *or* signs and wonders?

The kingdom of God, however, is not an either/or but a both/and kind of kingdom. The Bible *and* the Holy Spirit. Thinking *and* feeling. Teaching *and* experiencing. Preaching the gospel *and* signs and wonders. It's tragic that this topic often divides Christians and plunges them into an either/or mindset about the Holy Spirit. It's also ironic, because one of the key reasons Jesus sent the Holy Spirit was to unify believers in peace, not fuel divisiveness (see John 14:27).

Paul offered these stern words for those who divide: "Watch out for those who cause divisions and put obstacles in your way that are contrary to the teaching you have learned. Keep away from them. For such people are not serving our Lord Christ, but their own appetites. By smooth talk and flattery they deceive the minds of naive people" (Romans 16:17–18).

Jude wrote that those who were causing divisions in his day "follow mere natural instincts and do not have the Spirit" (verse 19). These individuals might have claimed to have the Holy Spirit, but their actions were proving they were not being led by him.

We avoid such division by being in union with God and other believers. As Paul writes, "I appeal to you, brothers and sisters, in the name of our Lord Jesus Christ, that all of you agree with one another in what you say and that there be no divisions among you, but that you be perfectly united in mind and thought" (1 Corinthians 1:10). This might sound foreign to us because we live in a divisive world, but the church should stand as a beacon of unity. This is not just wishful thinking—it's God's both/and kingdom!

Read: Romans 16:17–19; 1 Corinthians 1:10; Jude 1:17–19

1. When have you recently had to make a tough either/or choice? How did it play out?

2. In Romans 16:17–19, Paul doesn't just name divisiveness as a problem in the church but also describes what fuels it. What does he say some are doing to cause divisions? How does he describe those people who are actively engaged in doing this?

Certain churches major on teaching the Bible thoughtfully, intellectually, and exegetically, but the experience of the Holy Spirit is largely absent. Other churches major on the ecstatic experiences attributed to the Holy Spirit but tend to diminish the Bible to a shallow script for spiritual pep talks. . . . The church of Jesus Christ is a people who together emphatically declare, "Yes to the Holy Bible!" and in the same breath, "Yes to the Holy Spirit!" "Yes" to the intimate presence and supernatural power of a God who wants to be with us and even within us.[11]

3. What are some key signs that reveal whether a church is operating as an "either/or" or "both/and" community in terms of the Holy Spirit?

4. Jude says those who divide have two traits—they follow something and they lack someone (see verse 19). What are those two defining traits? How do they play into each other?

> To ignore the role of the devil who sows weeds in the night is to attempt to bring about a rich harvest from my inner life without cultivating the soil. To obsess over the devil, blaming our spiritual enemy for every stubbed toe and twist of fate, is to ignore the flesh and the world, again attempting to bring about a rich harvest from my inner life without cultivating the soil. Rather than ignoring or obsessing over the devil, we should "test the spirits to see whether they are from God" (1 John 4:1).[12]

5. When you look at the world today, do you think it is possible for believers in Christ to actually live in the unity that Paul describes in 1 Corinthians 1:10? What role would the Holy Spirit need to play in believers' lives for this to happen?

CATCH UP AND READ AHEAD

Connect with a group member this week to talk about some of the insights from this session. Use any of the prompts below to guide your discussion.

- Why is the Holy Spirit a "familiar stranger" to many Christians?
- What is your current relationship with the Holy Spirit?
- Which topics from this session resonated with you most? Why?
- How would you define *experiential spirituality*?
- What is your biggest hope for this study?
- What obstacles are in the way of this hope becoming a reality?

Use this time to complete any of the personal study and reflection questions from previous days that you weren't able to finish. Make a note below of any questions that you've had or significant insights and breakthroughs that you've gained.

Read chapters 2–4 in *The Familiar Stranger* before the next group session. Use the space below to make note of anything that stands out to you or encourages you.

WEEK 2

BEFORE GROUP MEETING	Read chapters 2–4 in *The Familiar Stranger* Read the Welcome section (page 20)
GROUP MEETING	Discuss the Connect questions Watch the video teaching for session 2 Discuss the questions that follow as a group Do the closing exercise and pray (pages 20–24)
STUDY 1	Complete the personal study (pages 26–28)
STUDY 2	Complete the personal study (pages 29–31)
STUDY 3	Complete the personal study (pages 32–34)
CATCH UP AND READ AHEAD (BEFORE WEEK 3 GROUP MEETING)	Connect with someone in your group Read chapter 7 in *The Familiar Stranger* Complete any unfinished personal studies (page 35)

THE PERSON OF THE HOLY SPIRIT

" Our explicit knowledge is the way we know God intellectually. Our implicit knowledge is the way we know God relationally and experientially."

A. W. TOZER, *THE KNOWLEDGE OF THE HOLY*[13]

WELCOME | READ ON YOUR OWN

In the first session, we looked at how the Holy Spirit is a "familiar stranger" to many Christians. He is *familiar* in the sense that his name appears in the Bible. But he is a *stranger* in that many have little to no idea of how he works in their lives. As a result, we end up with those who view the Holy Spirit as an impersonal power source and those who ignore him altogether.

What we need is a *reintroduction* to the person of the Holy Spirit. It's easy for us to assume the Holy Spirit—along with Jesus—stepped onto the scene in the New Testament. But that is incorrect. The Holy Spirit is actually present throughout the Old Testament—starting in the opening creation scene, where, in Genesis 1:2, the Spirit is actively hovering over the chaos to help fill it with beauty, life, and order.

So, to see what we may have previously missed, we'll look at five biblical scenes—both Old and New Testament—with fresh eyes. We'll explore the person of the Holy Spirit through the categories of Creation, Roots, Jesus, Then, and Now. Along the way, it will become clear how the words *tabernacle* and *temple* don't just refer to a building. You'll also discover how to experience the person of the Holy Spirit through the help of three key ingredients: a theology (what Scripture teaches); a model (a shared way for us to express beliefs); and a practice (a safe place where it's okay to learn, try, and even fail together).

All the way from creation to now, the Holy Spirit makes the impractical practice-able. By the Spirit, the ministry of Jesus is not only accessible to "super-spiritual" people but is available and practice-able for ordinary people who "tabernacle" with an extraordinary God. That's enough preview. Let's get to know the Holy Spirit together!

CONNECT | 10 MINUTES

If you or any of your group members don't know each other, take a few minutes to introduce yourselves. Then discuss one or both of the following questions:

- What is something that spoke to you from last week's personal study?

  — *or* —

- How are relational encounters with the Holy Spirit different from knowledge about the Spirit? Is one more important than the other?

WATCH | 25 MINUTES

Now watch the video for this session. Below is an outline of the key points covered during the teaching. Record any key concepts that stand out to you.

OUTLINE

I. **Creation: The Holy Spirit in Creation**
   A. God made a woman from Adam's side (see Genesis 2:20–22).
   B. The Hebrew word *tsela* is used for Adam's side and doesn't mean "rib."
   C. In almost every biblical occurrence, *tsela* refers to "tabernacle" or "temple."

II. **Roots: The Holy Spirit in the Old Testament**
   A. Throughout Exodus, God's presence is described as a dense cloud.
   B. God's presence fills the tent of meeting, the tabernacle, and eventually the temple.
   C. The tabernacle is good but incomplete.

III. **Jesus: How He Presents the Holy Spirit in the Gospels**
   A. John describes Jesus as a tabernacle filled with God's glory (presence).
   B. Jesus goes around acting like he *is* the tabernacle.
   C. When Jesus said, "Destroy this temple, and I will raise it again in three days" (John 2:19), he wasn't talking about a building but his body . . . and the Holy Spirit.

IV. **Then: The Life of the Spirit in the Early Church**
   A. Jesus breathes on his disciples and says, "Receive the Holy Spirit" (John 20:22).
   B. He then commissions them (see John 20:23).
   C. The church, filled by the Holy Spirit, should look like a continuation of what Jesus started.

V. **Now: The Holy Spirit's Invitation to Us**
   A. Paul says our bodies are temples, the dwelling place of God through the Holy Spirit (see 1 Corinthians 6:19–20).
   B. We are personally and individually filled with the very Spirit that filled Jesus.
   C. To experience this, we need a *theology*, a *model*, and a *practice*.

NOTES

DISCUSS | 35 MINUTES

Discuss what you just watched by answering the following questions.

1. In Genesis 2:20–22, God makes a woman from Adam's rib. The word translated "rib" (*tsela*) doesn't literally mean "rib" but the side of sacred architecture—usually a temple or tabernacle. What does this signify about Adam's and Eve's bodies—and thus our bodies?

2. God tells Moses to build a sanctuary for him and says, "I will dwell among them" (Exodus 25:8). Why is this such a revolutionary thought? How does it radically differ from the way people viewed other gods in that day?

3. From Moses to King Solomon, the theme of a tabernacle/temple emerges in the Old Testament. Why is what the tabernacle/temple represented good? Why is it incomplete?

4. Paul writes, "Do you not know that your bodies are temples of the Holy Spirit who is in you, whom you have received from God?" How do these words reflect the Holy Spirit's ongoing presence, harkening all the way back to creation?

5. What are some tangible ways the church today can be a continuation of every-thing that Jesus started? What part is the Holy Spirit empowering you to play?

RESPOND | 10 MINUTES

One of the reasons Jesus got in trouble with the religious authorities of his day was because he regularly did things you weren't supposed to do outside of the temple. He didn't require his followers to go through a cleansing ritual, offer sacrifices, or interact with a priest. He simply asked, "Do you want to repent? Okay. You're forgiven." Jesus went around acting like he *was* the tabernacle because he *is* the new tabernacle. Later in his ministry, he pushed this claim even further. While standing on the Temple Mount, he responded to his critics with these bold words:

> Jesus answered them, "Destroy this temple, and I will raise it again in three days." They replied, "It has taken forty-six years to build this temple, and you are going to raise it in three days?" But the temple he had spoken of was his body.
>
> JOHN 2:19–21

Why were the religious leaders so enraged at Jesus for forgiving sins and healing people outside of the temple system? Where do you see similar outrage today?

Jesus' body is the living, breathing, walking, talking temple. How does Jesus now fully embody what the tabernacle and temple represented in the Old Testament?

PRAY | 10 MINUTES

As you close, pray that you will come to know the Holy Spirit more deeply. Commit to not being satisfied by mere facts and stories about him but that you will seek to know him more fully as a unique person. Also ask to be known to him. Pray that he will work within you and re-create you from the inside out—reshaping you into God's original design for your life.

PERSONAL STUDY

The focus of this second session is on the person of the Holy Spirit. During your group time, you looked at five biblical scenes (Old and New Testament) to see how the theme of tabernacle/temple helps illuminate key aspects of what it means to be filled with the Spirit. This personal study portion is designed to take you—through stories and Scripture—deeper into the *person* the Holy Spirit. After the readings, look up the passages indicated and write down your responses to the questions. If you're part of a group, you will be given a few minutes to share your insights at the start of the next session. If you are reading *The Familiar Stranger* alongside this study, first review chapters 2–4 of the book.

STUDY 1

A PARTICULAR KIND OF TEACHER

There's a worldwide traveling stage show based on C. S. Lewis's classic allegory *The Screwtape Letters*. It spectacularly brings to life the book that was first published in 1942. The fictional story is told through a series of letters from a higher-ranking devil named Screwtape to his young protégé, Wormwood. The satirical approach creatively illuminates the ultimate power and goodness of God.

While creative liberties are taken with the costumes, set design, and choice of excerpts, the show is faithful to the source material written more than eighty years ago. The actor doesn't speak his own words or in his own authority. His voice declares the words of the creator of the content. It's the best decision the producer could have made because people come to hear and remember the words of C. S. Lewis.

When Jesus spoke his final words to his disciples, he shared these thoughts: "All this I have spoken while still with you. But the Advocate, the Holy Spirit, whom the Father will send in my name, will teach you all things and will remind you of everything I have said to you" (John 14:25–26). Later in the same conversation, Jesus added: "He will not speak on his own . . . the Spirit will receive from me what he will make known to you" (John 16:13, 15).

According to Jesus, the Holy Spirit is a particular kind of teacher: one who helps us remember. The Holy Spirit has no "original content." The ministry of the Holy Spirit is entirely about translating the teachings and promises of Jesus in a way that forms us at the deepest level—rewriting our neural pathways and enabling us to embody our redemption. The Holy Spirit pushes the teachings of Jesus from the head, where they can be understood, down into the heart, where they can heal our emotions and become a new foundation for us to live from.

The Holy Spirit is the conduit of spiritual experience. That's why he was sent to everyone in the upper room (see Acts 2:4)—as well as to us today.

Read: John 14:25–26; John 16:13, 15; Acts 2:4

1. Jesus' words in John 14:25–26 reveal aspects of the Holy Spirit's role. Why does Jesus call the Holy Spirit "the Advocate"? In whose name did the Father send the Holy Spirit?

2. In that same passage, Jesus identified two essential roles of the Holy Spirit. What are they? How are they distinct?

> Jesus teaches that God is a Father [of a prodigal son] running out to meet me, clothe me in royal robes, and welcome me to the home I wandered away from before I really knew what I was leaving. The Spirit makes this real to me. As high as the heavens are above the earth, that's how great God's love is for those who fear him. The Spirit helps us experience that love. As far as the east is from the west, that's how far he has removed our transgressions from us (see Psalm 103:11–12).[14]

3. According to Jesus, the Holy Spirit is a specific kind of teacher: one who helps you *remember*. In light of this, how is the Spirit currently rewriting your neural pathways to comprehend God's reality—and yourself—in new ways?

4. People often speak on their own authority, basing their power on their title or position. Write down below your titles and positions (work, church, family, and the like). Then, across from each title/position, write down the authority (God, company, church, parent/spouse, and the like) from which you speak in that role.

Your Title/Position	Authority

Now read John 16:13, 15. What does Jesus say about the authority the Holy Spirit speaks from? Specifically, what will the Spirit do—and not do?

The Hebrew word often translated as "know" or "knowledge" is *yada*. But this doesn't refer only to intellectual understanding. . . . In the Hebrew imagination, something wasn't known until it was understood relationally and experientially. *Yada* is a relational, experiential kind of knowledge. The Holy Spirit was given that you may know—experientially and relationally—the true life of everything Jesus taught.[15]

5. The Holy Spirit is the conduit of spiritual experience. A *conduit* is a channel connecting one source to another. Where do you feel disconnected from God right now? Will you ask for the Holy Spirit's help in repairing that connection?

STUDY 2

THE EMPOWERING AGENT

We're drawn to before-and-after stories. Those words—*before* and *after*—are two of the most powerful bookends to any situation or event because we know we're about to hear a tale of something or someone that was radically one way and is now radically another way. Like life before—and then after—the invention of electricity or air-conditioning. Or those before-and-after testimonials that show the radical transformation of a person's life.

But the greatest "before and after" belongs to those who give their lives to Jesus. More than a transformation, they describe their "after" as being reborn.

Even Jesus experienced a before-and-after moment—one that directly involves the Holy Spirit. *Before* his baptism, where the Holy Spirit descended on him "like a dove" (John 1:32 NKJV), Jesus lived thirty years, and as far as we know he didn't utter a word of teaching, work a miracle, or recruit a disciple. *After* his baptism, Jesus was constantly teaching, working miracles, and calling disciples. His baptism was the inciting incident that started it all.

The historic belief of the church and the clear biblical evidence is that the supernatural power of Jesus came through the Holy Spirit. Peter remembered it this way: "You know what has happened throughout the province of Judea, beginning in Galilee after the baptism that John preached—how God anointed Jesus of Nazareth with the Holy Spirit and power, and how he went around doing good and healing" (Acts 10:37–38).

This understanding of the Holy Spirit as the empowering agent of Jesus' ministry is so essential because what started with Jesus didn't stop with Jesus. Scripture plainly states that the same Spirit who anointed Jesus anoints all who receive Jesus as Lord and Savior (see 2 Corinthians 1:21–22). We have the same empowering agent—the Holy Spirit—who is ready to change our "before and after" reality in tangible, practical, and miraculous ways.

Read: John 1:32–33; Acts 10:37–38; 2 Corinthians 1:21–22

1. In our culture, we tend to hear far more about self-empowerment than about the Holy Spirit being our empowering agent. Why do you think that is the case?

2. How does viewing the Holy Spirit's role in the baptism of Jesus (see John 1:32–33) as not just God's validation but the "inciting incident" of his power change your perception of this major "before and after" moment in Jesus' life?

Luke opens the book of Acts with the line, "In my former book, Theophilus, I wrote about all that Jesus *began* to do and to teach" (1:1, emphasis added). The implication, of course, being that this book is about what Jesus *continued* to do and teach. Only this book isn't about the life of Jesus. It's about the lives of his followers continuing all that he started. And in the second chapter of Acts, in an upper room in Jerusalem where the disciples had gathered to wait according to Jesus' instructions, the Spirit descended and rested on each of them. Said another way, they were anointed at Pentecost by the very Spirit that anointed Jesus at his baptism.[16]

3. In Acts 10:37–38, Peter makes a clear distinction of what Jesus did *after* as compared to *before* his baptism. What did Jesus do *after* his baptism? By whose power was Jesus anointed to do those things?

4. Read 2 Corinthians 1:21–22. What started with Jesus didn't stop with Jesus. How is the Holy Spirit referred to in this passage? What does that mean to you?

Jesus, looking ahead to the gift of the Spirit, claimed, "Very truly I tell you, whoever believes in me will do the works I have been doing, and they will do even greater things than these, because I am going to the Father" (John 14:12). Jesus is plainly telling us that "whoever believes in me will do my very works by my very Spirit." The apostle John later summarized, "But you have an anointing from the Holy One" (1 John 2:20). Every follower of Jesus has been anointed with the very Spirit that anointed Jesus at his baptism and empowered his ministry.[17]

---

5. We tend to be more aware of the "before and after" that happens when we invite Jesus into our hearts than we are aware of the Holy Spirit's impact on us. What are some ways the "empowering agent" has changed your life through his power and presence?

My Life Before the Holy Spirit	My Life After the Holy Spirit

If you found it difficult to offer specific "after" examples, take a moment to ask the Holy Spirit to reveal how he is working in your life. What is his response?

STUDY 3

FROM BELIEF TO PRACTICE

The man lived on the outskirts of a village, in the crevice of a cliff. He admired the cottages below but didn't have the tools or the knowledge to make one. And even if he did, he couldn't do it alone. One day a stranger appeared and asked the man why he was sad. "I desire a home, sir," the man replied. "But I don't know the foundational principles of building one, nor do I have a community to model it and help me practice and push through my mistakes."

"My friend," the stranger said, "how could you know if no one's shown you? I'm a carpenter, and I trained those who built the houses below. Come with me, follow my ways, and you'll experience the joy of creating a home with others."

This is the struggle of many faithful followers of Jesus. We're held back in the ministry of the Spirit not by a lack of desire but by a lack of practice. We do not know how or where to start. We believe God speaks today, heals today, and delivers today, but no one has given us a healthy model of how to do the same. As John Wimber noted, "For anything to be picked up off the pages of Scripture and lived in a local community within a particular context, three ingredients are needed: a theology, a model, and a practice."[18]

A *theology* means a common understanding of what the Bible teaches about a topic. As Paul wrote, "The things you have heard me say in the presence of many witnesses entrust to reliable people who will also be qualified to teach others" (2 Timothy 2:2). Next, a *model* translates the expression of a belief in a way that fits a people and a place. Paul demonstrated this approach while in Rome: "To the weak I became weak, to win the weak. I have become all things to all people so that by all possible means I might save some" (1 Corinthians 9:22).

Finally, we need a *safe space* to practice where it is okay to fail as we learn the mechanics of that model together. Proverbs 1:5 puts it this way: "Let the wise listen and add to their learning, and let the discerning get guidance." That is how we start. And how we grow.

Read: 2 Timothy 2:2; 1 Corinthians 9:22; Proverbs 1:5

1. Many Christians have never been given a healthy model for supernatural experiences or practices. Can you recall a time you felt held back in the ministry of the Spirit—not by a lack of desire but by a lack of practice—and did not know how or where to start? What was most lacking for you at that time?

> How could someone like me receive so much pastoral training and never be given a healthy model for supernatural practice? And I'm not trying to pass the buck here, either, as if this were just a failure of my teachers and leaders. Equally troubling is the fact that I had read Scripture prayerfully every morning for approximately half my life at that point—particularly the Gospels where Jesus heals frequently and likewise sends his disciples out to heal. And never once had I given healing prayer a real shot.[19]

2. To have a common understanding of what Scripture teaches, why is it necessary to spend time with reliable people who are qualified to teach others (see 2 Timothy 2:2) rather than just try to figure it out on your own?

3. Proverbs 1:5 contains a generous invitation for both experts and beginners. What is the offer to the wise? What about to those who discern they need help? Which category most describes you when it comes to the Holy Spirit?

Practice is protected space where the stakes are lowered because it's not the performance, game, or recital. Instead, we are working together so that we all grow together through shared practice. That is the definition of practice I have in mind—one aimed not at individual mastery but more mature, shared ministry. . . . However, when it comes to gifts of the Spirit, like prophecy or healing, for example, most churches do not have space for practice. This creates the false belief that a gift of healing is for the uber-anointed world traveler and prophecy is for the holy weirdo with dreams and visions rather than the ordinary disciple in the local church. If we want today's churches to look like the ancient churches that set the world on fire, we must practice as those early communities practiced. We do this through setting aside intentional spaces of training in the various gifts and expressions of the Spirit, which are designed to form us into empty channels through which the Spirit's power flows on earth as in heaven.[20]

4. Do you have a protected space within a church community where the stakes have been lowered and everyone can grow through shared practice in the various gifts and expressions of the Spirit? Why is having a safe space to practice so crucial for spiritual growth?

5. On a scale of 1 (lowest) to 10 (highest), list where you feel you are in the three key areas of *theology*, *model*, and *practice* as described in the reading.

Theology	Model	Practice
____	____	____

How did you choose those specific ratings for each of the three categories?

CATCH UP AND READ AHEAD

Connect with a group member this week to talk about some of the insights from this session. Use any of the prompts below to guide your discussion.

- Which topics from this session resonated with you the most? Why?
- How is experiencing the Spirit different from intellectual knowledge?
- What stood out to you about the Holy Spirit's role in creation?
- Why do many people see the Holy Spirit as a force rather than a person?
- How would you like the Holy Spirit to make the impractical practice-able?
- What question would you most like to ask the Holy Spirit today?

Use this time to complete any of the personal study and reflection questions from previous days that you weren't able to finish. Make a note below of any questions that you've had or significant insights and breakthroughs that you've gained.

Read chapter 7 in *The Familiar Stranger* before the next group session. Use the space below to make note of anything that stands out to you or encourages you.

WEEK 3

BEFORE GROUP MEETING	Read chapter 7 in *The Familiar Stranger* Read the Welcome section (page 38)
GROUP MEETING	Discuss the Connect questions Watch the video teaching for session 3 Discuss the questions that follow as a group Do the closing exercise and pray (pages 38–42)
STUDY 1	Complete the personal study (pages 44–46)
STUDY 2	Complete the personal study (pages 47–49)
STUDY 3	Complete the personal study (pages 50–52)
CATCH UP AND READ AHEAD (BEFORE WEEK 4 GROUP MEETING)	Connect with someone in your group Read chapter 8 in *The Familiar Stranger* Complete any unfinished personal studies (page 53)

DISCERNMENT

" *The art of discernment is both central to the Christian life today and, at the same time, not very well understood even by prayerful and committed Christians.* "

THOMAS GREEN, *WEEDS AMONG THE WHEAT*[21]

WELCOME | READ ON YOUR OWN

After familiarizing ourselves with the person of the Holy Spirit, we'll now look at some of the expressions of the Spirit—starting with the gift of discernment.

To hear and live by God's voice is one of the most potent and most dangerous aspects of Christian spirituality. Nothing matters more than learning to discern God's voice, and yet few things are more susceptible to pain, abuse, delusion, and deception. There's nothing more beautiful than being guided by the Spirit in ways that bless us and defy human explanation. But what about the times when we cry out to God and only hear silence in return? Or when an authority figure betrays us by misrepresenting the Holy Spirit and misusing God's Word?

Seasons of blessing are wonderful. But how do we interpret the seasons of silence or what feels like abandonment? The pull may be to play it safe and walk away from experiential spirituality. And while that may, at least on the surface, reduce risk, it also keeps us from all that God has to offer. What's needed in these moments isn't more control but greater clarity. Which is exactly what the Holy Spirit wants to give us.

Discernment is the gift and practice of attuning to God's voice amid the competing, counterfeit noises. In this session, we'll explore why we tend to miss God in our midst, how we can grow in discernment both individually and in community, and how to discern the voice of God from the other voices vying for our attention—the world, the flesh, and the devil. Discernment isn't a puzzle for us to solve. It's a gift of the Spirit, allowing us to be led by the Good Shepherd who knows us, loves us, and desires to guide us home.

CONNECT | 10 MINUTES

Get the session started by choosing one or both of the following questions to discuss together as a group:

- What is something that spoke to you from last week's personal study?

  — or —

- Describe a time you asked God for guidance, heard his voice, and things came together in a way beyond anything you could have done in your own strength. Is this your normal experience or the exception?

WATCH | 25 MINUTES

Now watch the video for this session. Below is an outline of the key points covered during the teaching. Record any key concepts that stand out to you.

OUTLINE

I. God's Voice and Direction
  A. Sometimes we clearly hear God's voice, and the results validate this reality.
  B. Sometimes we cry out to God, and he seemingly says nothing back.
  C. Sometimes we are hurt by the misuse of God's Word by an authority figure.

II. The Gift of Discernment
  A. One of the primary aims of spiritual growth is to become a "prudent money changer."
  B. We become so familiar with God's voice that we can quickly spot a counterfeit voice.
  C. Discernment is the gift and practice of attuning to God's voice in the midst of the competing noise.

III. The Theology of Discernment
  A. Discerning God's voice in our lives begins by recognizing it in the lives of those in the Bible.
  B. God himself passed right by the majority of people who saw him or heard his voice.
  C. God's native language is a whisper, which is hard to hear and easy to ignore.
  D. The primary voices vying for our attention are the world, the flesh, and the devil.

IV. The Model of Discernment
  A. Recognize the difference between God's whispers and the deceiver's lies.
  B. Observe what the voice we're hearing does to us as we listen to it.
  C. Remember the battle is between the ego (shallow hungers) and the soul (deep longings).

V. The Practice of Discernment
  A. Discernment works less like a prescription and more like a daily vitamin.
  B. Discernment is both an individual and a communal practice.
  C. Discernment in community comes through three types of relationships: spiritual friendships, spiritual direction, and formal group discernment.

NOTES

DISCUSS | 35 MINUTES

Discuss what you just watched by answering the following questions.

1. Discernment is the gift and practice of attuning to God's voice amid the competing, counterfeit noises. Do you agree that nothing matters more than learning to discern the voice of God? Why or why not?

2. In your own words, summarize the concept of the "prudent money changer." How does this relate to spiritual maturity and our ability to discern God's voice?

3. When Jesus was on the road to Emmaus, the two disciples didn't recognize him (see Luke 24:13–16). What are the main reasons you tend to miss Jesus when he is in your midst?

4. John makes this statement about Jesus in his Gospel: "He was in the world, and though the world was made through him, the world did not recognize him" (1:10). What counterfeit images of Jesus does the world hold that make his true presence unrecognizable?

5. The primary competing voices to God's whisper are the world, the flesh, and the devil. Which of these three most often trips you up? Why?

RESPOND | 10 MINUTES

One of the most memorable moments in the Old Testament was when Elijah called fire down from heaven. But his story didn't end at that high point. Following the standoff against the prophets of Baal, Elijah became a wanted man. After forty days in the wilderness, he climbed Mount Horeb, where the word of the Lord came to him.

> "Go out and stand on the mountain in the presence of the LORD, for the LORD is about to pass by." Then a great and powerful wind tore the mountains apart and shattered the rocks before the LORD, but the LORD was not in the wind. After the wind there was an earthquake, but the LORD was not in the earthquake. After the earthquake came a fire, but the LORD was not in the fire. And after the fire came a gentle whisper.
>
> 1 KINGS 19:11-12

Don't overlook this phrase: "Go out and stand on the mountain in the presence of the LORD, for the LORD is about to pass by." What if we could hear God not just on top of Mount Horeb but in our everyday moments?

Pete Greig writes, "If we are ever to feel fully safe and truly loved by the Lord of all the earth, we must . . . learn to listen for his voice in the anticlimax of life's nonevents."[22] What does it mean to listen for God's voice in the "anticlimax of life's nonevents"?

God's voice came to Elijah not through the wind, the earthquake, or the fire but in a gentle whisper. How do you tend to look for God to speak in big ways through major events and esteemed people rather than in the quiet of a normal morning?

PRAY | 10 MINUTES

Pray that God will show you how to hear him and live by his voice. Ask him to remind you that he is not silent but often speaks in a whisper. Pray that he will teach you to discern his voice from the competing noise of the world, the flesh, and the devil. Ask for him to open your eyes and ears so you won't miss him as he passes by.

PERSONAL STUDY

The focus of this third session is on the Holy Spirit's gift of discernment. During your group time, you explored examples of those who heard God's voice in the Bible, learned what distracts you from hearing his voice today, and discovered ways to grow in this essential aspect of your faith. This personal study portion is designed to take you—through stories and Scripture—deeper into these topics. After the readings, look up the passages indicated and write down your responses to the questions. If you're part of a group, you will be given a few minutes to share your insights at the start of the next session. If you are reading *The Familiar Stranger* alongside this study, first review chapter 7 of the book.

STUDY 1

CULTIVATE YOUR SOUL

A lush green lawn—whether in a yard or on a golf course—is a beauty to behold. But it doesn't happen naturally, especially in drier regions of the world. A lawn like that has to be *cultivated*. The process starts in the unseen places. The dirt must be broken up or loosened so that vital nutrients and air can access and enrich the soil. Proper care also includes knowing when and how much to water and limiting the infiltration of weeds so they don't overtake the lawn.

The concept of cultivating the ground goes all the way back to Genesis, where God placed Adam in the garden of Eden to care for it and to tend it (see Genesis 2:15).

In Matthew 13:24-29, Jesus describes a wheat field the enemy sets out to sabotage with weeds. The parable is a description of the harvest at the end of the age, but it's also a metaphor for our inner world, where weeds and wheat grow together. There really is an indwelling Holy Spirit speaking life, clarity, and direction into believers to produce a rich harvest. And there really is an enemy scheming to sow lies and confusion into the life of every believer and spoiling (or, at the very least, choking and diminishing) the harvest in our souls.

Ignoring the role of the devil, who sows weeds, is to attempt to bring about a rich harvest from our inner lives without cultivating the soil. Obsessing over the devil, blaming him for every stubbed toe and twist of fate, is to ignore the flesh and the world—which again results in attempting to bring about a rich harvest from our inner lives without cultivating the soil. Instead of ignoring or obsessing over the devil, we should "test the spirits to see whether they are from God" (1 John 4:1).

It takes intention, time, and consistency to cultivate soil. The same holds true for cultivating our soul.

Read: Genesis 2:15; Matthew 13:24-29; 1 John 4:1

1. Why do you think God gave Adam the responsibility to cultivate the garden of Eden (see Genesis 2:15) when he could have made the soil self-sustaining or just done it himself? Likewise, why does God require you to cultivate your soul?

2. In Jesus' parable of the wheat field in Matthew 13:24–29, the weeds don't randomly appear but are the work of a crafty enemy trying to sabotage the soil. How does knowing this change your response to the lies and confusion trying to diminish the harvest of your soul?

Because the inner life of the believer is like the field that contains both God's wheat and the enemy's weeds, the process of hearing and keeping in step with the Spirit involves attentiveness to the inner dynamics and movements of the soul. The Spirit's whisper is directed at the soul's depths, while the deceiver's lies appeal to the shallow waters of the ego. . . . The key to discerning between the Holy Spirit's whisper and the deceiver's scheme starts with recognizing what the voice is doing to you as you listen to it. What part of you is being inflamed by this inner voice—your shallow hungers or your deep longings, your ego or your soul? Discernment is, in large part, the spiritual practice of differentiating between the listening ear of your ego and your soul.[23]

3. John says to "test the spirits" (1 John 4:1). How do the concepts of *hunger* and *longing* add clarity when trying to discern between the Spirit's whisper and the deceiver's schemes?

4. Why is it counterproductive to either *ignore* or *obsess* over the role of the devil? How can either response keep you from cultivating the soil of your soul?

We are forever tempted toward self-absorption. We imagine ourselves at the center of the story, and in so doing we dethrone Jesus and confuse the voice of the Good Shepherd with an imposter. What is broadly known today as "the ego" Scripture most often names "the flesh." The flesh is where competing desires take root within the individual person, getting all the way into our personality structure and thought patterns—ambition, insecurity, perfectionism, and the like. All of these are not bad on their own, but they do serve as competing voices to the Spirit's whisper. For example, a propensity toward ambition may make hearing a call to a more hidden, uncelebrated role more difficult for a driven individual to recognize as the Spirit's voice offering life.[24]

5. In the left circle, write your name in the center and then list the people and events of your life around the perimeter. In the right, do the same except replace your name with the name *Jesus*. In which circle will the imposter have less authority to sabotage? Why?

STUDY 2

SELF-DISCERNMENT METER

Culture has convinced us there's no greater good than self-care, self-help, and being a self-made person. We're now taking it even further. We genuinely think we're good at self-awareness. We're not. Our self-discernment meter is broken.

Usually, we place our validation in our accomplishments. We justify our actions without considering why we react in certain ways. In most areas of life, we tend to believe we're right. If our annual work reviews or school finals ever suddenly changed to self-evaluations, we'd all get A's and immediate promotions. But our self-discernment meter can also swing to the other end of the spectrum. We secretly doubt our worth. Some days, we feel disposable and invisible rather than, as Scripture says, God's handiwork (see Ephesians 2:10).

None of us have completely accurate perceptions of ourselves or a perfect read on our inner dynamics and motivations. Reaching all the way back to Eden, life in communion with God has always involved living in community with others, and attunement to God's voice has always required community in order for its members to mature to their full potential. As author Jared Patrick Boyd says, "Discernment in community means that we're doing the work of noticing and nurturing the presence of God's activity with and for one another."[25]

Spiritual friendship is one type of relationship through which we can experience discernment. It requires us to intentionally invite another person—the kind Proverbs 18:24 describes as one who sticks closer than a brother—into our sense of the Spirit's whisper and ask them to refine our attention and response. It involves deep, prayerful listening and asking questions more often than offering direction or advice. It demands deep trust and complete vulnerability, and it can be experienced only between people with a shared commitment to (and existing practice of) individual discernment.

And . . . it's a beautiful antidote to our broken self-discernment meter.

Read: Romans 12:3; Ephesians 2:10; Proverbs 18:24

1. Do you think it's true that no person has completely accurate self-perception or a perfect read on their own inner dynamics and motivations? Why or why not?

2. To practice spiritual friendship, do you have a friend who is closer than a brother (see Proverbs 18:24)? If not, what would it require of you to be that kind of friend to someone?

> Discernment in community . . . comes through three types of relationships: spiritual friendship, spiritual direction, and formal group discernment. Spiritual direction is more formal than spiritual friendship, practiced individually with a qualified sacred listener. When searching for a spiritual director, seek out a seasoned believer who is well-trained in the art of holy listening and committed to a local church community. Because discernment matures in community, beware of a spiritual director who is untethered to a church community and fostering their own ongoing process of maturing spiritually.[26]

3. Spiritual direction is another kind of relationship in which you can experience discernment. Would you be open to spiritual direction with a qualified sacred listener? Why or why not? If you've been to a spiritual director, did it lead to clarity or breakthrough?

4. In Romans 12:3, what does Paul tell us to do to increase our discernment and decrease our self-focus?

We will never reach a stage of spiritual maturity that allows us to practice discernment independently of community. Spiritual friendship, spiritual direction, and formal group discernment are not training wheels that we'll one day take off the bike when we feel really ready to ride. They're lifelong commitments. And that is not because God is playing it coy. It's because, to borrow the words of Genesis, "It is not good for [us] to be alone" (Genesis 2:18). We are meant to know and hear God within the context of community.[27]

---

5. Spiritual friendship, spiritual direction, and formal group discernment are meant to be lifelong commitments. On a scale of 1 (not happening) to 10 (fully participating), rate where you are in each of these three categories.

Spiritual friendship:

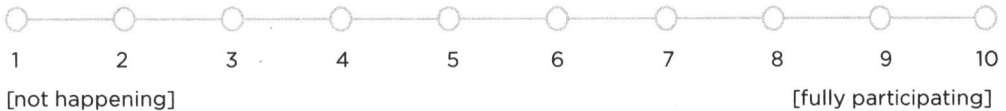

| 1 | 2 | 3 | 4 | 5 | 6 | 7 | 8 | 9 | 10 |

[not happening]   [fully participating]

Spiritual direction:

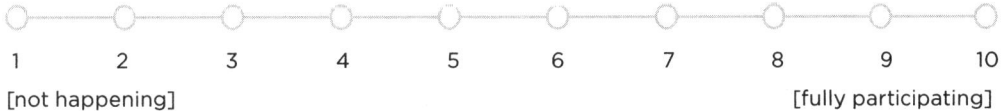

| 1 | 2 | 3 | 4 | 5 | 6 | 7 | 8 | 9 | 10 |

[not happening]   [fully participating]

Formal group discernment:

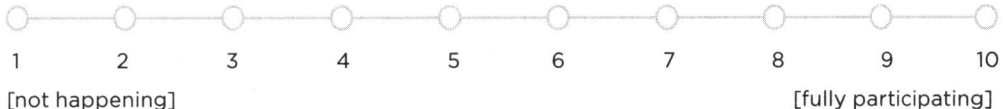

| 1 | 2 | 3 | 4 | 5 | 6 | 7 | 8 | 9 | 10 |

[not happening]   [fully participating]

STUDY 3

LOOK BACK TO SEE AHEAD

"Let the past stay in the past." "That was then—this is now." "I don't do yesterday." The past often gets a bad rap. It's seen as outdated. Or dismissed as a waste of time to focus on. After all, you can't head into your future looking backward. Or can you? While we are time-bound, God operates outside of time. Jesus is "the same yesterday and today and forever" (Hebrews 13:8). And often, God uses the past to help us see our present situation more clearly.

They say hindsight is 20/20, and that certainly applies to the way we navigate our spirituality. It's easier to perceive God's presence when we're looking back than it is in the moment. A good way to practice this is by praying the Prayer of Examen (or the "examination of conscience"), developed by Saint Ignatius. It typically involves five steps.

- **Gratitude:** Note the ways you have experienced God's loving presence today and thank the Giver for his gifts.
- **Ask:** Invite the Spirit to provide insight beyond human capacity.
- **Review:** Recap the day you've just lived in partnership with the Spirit, noting the experiences of God's nearness while also checking for the invitations you may have missed—moments when God passed right by, unnoticed or ignored.
- **Repentance:** Ask forgiveness for any moments you rejected, ignored, or rebelled against God's invitation to you.
- **Renewal:** Looking ahead to the next twenty-four hours, resolve to live in concert with God's direction.

As you learn to recognize God in hindsight, the most amazing thing happens. Slowly but surely, you learn to recognize God in the present—to know him not just at the dinner table in the evening but all along the road to Emmaus . . . to recognize him in those moments when "the Lord is about to pass by" (1 Kings 19:11).

Read: Hebrews 13:8; Jeremiah 33:3; 1 John 1:9

1. How do you feel about the past? In what ways might God be wanting to help you navigate what's next by reminding you of what's come before it?

2. Jesus is "the same yesterday and today and forever" (Hebrews 13:8). What does this reveal about Jesus' unchanging nature over time? How does it help you to know that the Jesus you read about in the Bible has the same qualities today?

> Author and professor Bobby Clinton argues that both Scripture and church history indicate that pretty much everything God speaks to us until around our sixties is preparation. If there's fruit, that's a bonus, but the aim is preparation and training in discernment—to learn God's voice and live with such radical trust that your life becomes an open channel between heaven and earth.[28]

3. The Prayer of Examen is a powerful practice for living an examined life. The first step involves seeing how you've experienced God's presence today and thanking him for his gift. The second step involves asking the Holy Spirit to provide insight beyond human capacity. In Jeremiah 33:3, what did God promise his people when they called out to him? How can this help you navigate what's ahead?

4. The third step in the Prayer of Examen involves recapping the day you've just lived in partnership with the Spirit. The fourth step requires repentance. First John 1:9 addresses this with a beautiful "if/then" promise. What must you do first? What will God then do?

The Prayer of Examen involves attunement to the inner life—mind, will, and emotions. It demands attentiveness to the whole person and cultivates emotional maturity as you review your day in terms of your thoughts, feelings, and motives. You can practice the Examen daily on your commute home from work or during a break from the responsibilities of your day. If alone, you can pray aloud, speaking directly to your Father in heaven. Take time to savor the day's blessings, recount your day with the Spirit's introspective aid, ask forgiveness, and pray intercession as God's mercy goes behind and before you.[29]

5. Take a few moments to practice going through all five steps of the Prayer of Examen. After each prompt below, write out a brief response or thought.

Gratitude	
Ask	
Review	
Repentance	
Renewal	

Which of the five steps did you find the most challenging? Why?

CATCH UP AND READ AHEAD

Connect with a group member this week to talk about some of the insights from this session. Use any of the prompts below to guide your discussion.

- What are your beliefs about hearing the voice of God?
- Why is God's native language usually a whisper?
- Which counterfeit voice derails you most—the world, the flesh, or the devil?
- Do you generally consider yourself a discerning person in spiritual matters?
- Are you more comfortable practicing discernment alone or in a group?
- What was your biggest "aha moment" about discernment this week?

Use this time to complete any of the personal study and reflection questions from previous days that you weren't able to finish. Make a note below of any questions that you've had or significant insights and breakthroughs that you've gained.

Read chapter 8 in *The Familiar Stranger* before the next group session. Use the space below to make note of anything that stands out to you or encourages you.

WEEK 4

BEFORE GROUP MEETING	Read chapter 8 in *The Familiar Stranger* Read the Welcome section (page 56)
GROUP MEETING	Discuss the Connect questions Watch the video teaching for session 4 Discuss the questions that follow as a group Do the closing exercise and pray (pages 56–60)
STUDY 1	Complete the personal study (pages 62–65)
STUDY 2	Complete the personal study (pages 65–68)
STUDY 3	Complete the personal study (pages 69–72)
CATCH UP AND READ AHEAD (BEFORE WEEK 5 GROUP MEETING)	Connect with someone in your group Read chapter 9 in *The Familiar Stranger* Complete any unfinished personal studies (page 73)

PROPHECY

"The primary role of the prophetic anointing
is to reveal God to the human heart."

DAVID FRITCH, *ENTHRONED*[30]

WELCOME | READ ON YOUR OWN

The realm of biblical prophecy can be a lightning-rod topic. Because of this, many churches and small groups choose to completely sidestep this spiritual gift altogether. But that's tragic.

The Spirit-empowered ministry of prophecy isn't limited to some elite group of super-spiritual leaders. It is a gift that all believers—children and seniors, men and women, rich and poor—should regularly experience. It simply means hearing and speaking a message from God that is directed to another individual or group.

Prophecy is not an optional sub-point in the biblical story. In fact, apart from prophecy, the biblical story can't be told. Prophecy is at the *heart* of the story—and it should be at the heart of our stories today. For these reasons, we need to understand what prophecy means biblically, communally, and practically. In doing so, we will discover answers to some of the biggest questions around the topic of prophecy, including:

- How do we live in line with the biblical picture of prophecy here and now?
- What are the three core aspects of prophetic prayer?
- How do we discern if we're hearing from God or if it's just in our heads?
- When we receive prophetic words, how can we tell if they're from God?
- What role does our imagination play—and should we ignore it?

If the foundation of our lives is biblical truth, the shape of our lives should be prophetic. It's meant to be a normal part of the Christian life. So, friends, why don't we give it a shot?

CONNECT | 10 MINUTES

Get the session started by choosing one or both of the following questions to discuss together as a group:

- What is something that spoke to you from last week's personal study?

  — *or* —

- Have you been the recipient of a prophetic word from someone? If so, what was that experience like for you?

WATCH | 25 MINUTES

Now watch the video for this session. Below is an outline of the key points covered during the teaching. Record any key concepts that stand out to you.

OUTLINE

I. The Gift of Prophecy
  A. Prophecy is hearing and speaking a message from God on behalf of another person.

  B. The gifts of the Spirit are not techniques or something you master—you receive them.

  C. The gift of prophecy is meant to be for all believers, not just a select few.

II. The Theology of Prophecy
  A. Creation was spoken into being by the *ruakh* ("breath" or "Spirit") of God.

  B. God's redemption strategy mirrors his creation strategy—he re-creates through his Spirit.

  C. The prophets of old experienced the gift of prophecy for specific moments. Now, Jesus has given us the Holy Spirit so we have constant access to this gift.

III. Prophecy in the Church
  A. When God's people gather, the assumption is he is speaking through them to one another.

  B. Believers in Christ are empowered by the Holy Spirit to strengthen, encourage, and comfort each other.

  C. Prophecy fosters connection and intimacy with God.

IV. The Practice of Prophecy
  A. Requires listening: revelation, interpretation, and application.

  B. Involves speaking: words that are affirming, biblical, and Christlike.

  C. Includes receiving: weighing it against Scripture, Jesus, and trust.

V. The Purpose and Power of Prophecy
  A. It pushes Jesus' teachings from the head to the heart.

  B. It transforms general truths into personal realities.

  C. It strengthens believers' faith through love and humility.

NOTES

DISCUSS | 35 MINUTES

Discuss what you just watched by answering the following questions.

1. From the creation of Adam and Eve, human beings were meant to be filled with God's Spirit. How did sin and the enemy steal God's breath from our lungs? How does God re-create us through his breath and Spirit?

2. What desire does Moses express in Numbers 11:29? What was his longing ultimately pointing to—and when did it become a reality?

3. Dallas Willard wrote, "If we look at . . . how the meetings of the church were supposed to proceed as given in 1 Corinthians 14, we see they assumed that numerous people in the congregation were going to have some kind of communication from God which they would be sharing with others in the group."[31] Why do you think this once-ordinary experience has become so rare today?

4. Learning to hear God's voice is not simple but requires uncomfortable risk. Are you personally willing to get it wrong to grow in this gift? Why or why not?

5. Prophecy isn't primarily about predicting the future, nor is it about us. True prophecy points to the person and teachings of Jesus. What does John 14:25–26 say regarding this? How does knowing this help you "test" a prophetic word?

RESPOND | 10 MINUTES

The longing for God to pour out his Spirit on all people is found throughout the Old Testament. The prophet Joel long ago described God's plan and declared it was coming in this passage:

> "I will pour out my Spirit on all people. Your sons and daughters will prophesy, your old men will dream dreams, your young men will see visions. Even on my servants, both men and women, I will pour out my Spirit in those days."
>
> JOEL 2:28-29

In 1 Corinthians 14:5, Paul wrote, "I would like every one of you . . . to prophesy." We all can prophesy because we have been filled with the Spirit. We now permanently carry what the prophets of old carried at particular times for particular purposes. The gift of prophecy is the ordinary practice of what was extraordinary before the risen Jesus breathed on all of us.

Joel says the day is coming when God will pour out his Spirit on all people. Now that we are in that time, why do you think we see so little fruit of this?

Joel's description of what will happen when the Spirit is poured out includes people making prophecies, having dreams, and seeing visions. Have you experienced any of these gifts? If so, which ones?

PRAY | 10 MINUTES

Invite the Holy Spirit to speak to you and give his messages to you on behalf of others. Pray that you will have eyes to see and ears to hear what he wants to say so you convey the love of Jesus clearly—not just as a general idea but as a personal reality that draws people to God. Ask for the courage to risk sharing what you hear from the Holy Spirit with others—and to receive from others what he has for you.

PERSONAL STUDY

The focus of this fourth session is on one of the Holy Spirit's most amazing gifts: *prophecy*. What does the Bible teach about it? How do you grow in your ability to hear, share, and receive prophetic words? Why is prophecy at the very heart of experiential spirituality? This personal study portion is designed to take you—through stories and Scripture—into a deeper exploration of these questions. After the readings, look up the passages indicated and write down your responses to the questions. If you're part of a group, you will be given a few minutes to share your insights at the start of the next session. If you are reading *The Familiar Stranger* alongside this study, first review chapter 8 of the book.

STUDY 1

THERE IS NO FORMULA

Life is unpredictable. Navigating constant change can be confusing. Staying hopeful in chaos is overwhelming. So we look for ways to control our days. When we find something that works, we lock in on it. If we just keep following the formula, we hope we'll get the same results while reducing risk. But God is not a God of formula. And the spiritual life isn't something we can manufacture in our own wisdom or strength. The only way to reduce risk is to humbly enter every aspect of our lives with God.

This is especially true when it comes to prophecy. Try as we might, we can't control the process. Prophecy involves hearing and speaking a message from God directed to another individual or group. *We* are not telling them what *we* think they should do, nor are *we* offering our opinion. As John writes, it is the Spirit who gives the words: "He will guide you into all the truth. He will not speak on his own; he will speak only what he hears, and he will tell you what is yet to come" (John 16:13).

Of course, for anyone who's ever tried to hear God, we know that our souls aren't automatically attuned to his voice. Experientially, God mostly makes himself available but not obvious, so hearing his voice takes some practice—and the uncomfortable risking we call *obedience*. As we read in Psalm 143:10, "Teach me to do your will, for you are my God; may your good Spirit lead me on level ground."

Jesus said that "his sheep follow him because they know his voice" (John 10:4). But how do we learn to hear the Shepherd's voice? We follow him. We ask God to speak to us, and then we walk in obedience, only half sure (at best) that it's God's voice we heard and not our own imagination. Mistakes will be made. Learning the Shepherd's voice requires risk and obedience.

There is no formula for this, only familiarity. We learn God's voice by risk, so we must be willing to get it wrong if we're going to get it right. As we take risks, the voice of God becomes more frequent and familiar. And, on the flip side, if we're not open to appearing foolish from time to time, we'll have a hard time following Jesus and learning the Shepherd's voice.

Read: John 16:13; John 10:4; Psalm 143:10

1. When you are the one looking to control the decisions of your life—including spiritual experiences—how can that get in the way of hearing God's voice?

2. Prophecy isn't you sharing your insights or wisdom with others but you hearing and speaking a message from God. According to John 16:13, does the Spirit model this particular aspect of the process for us?

The biggest barrier for the modern believer when it comes to prophecy is some version of, "Well, how do I know that's God and not just my imagination?" A good—and important—question. But to address the question, we must first correct the false dichotomy within the question. In the play *Saint Joan*, there's a scene that's both funny and insightful. Joan of Arc insists that she hears the voice of God. A skeptic says, "That's just your imagination." She responds, "I know. That's how God speaks to me."[32] . . . If God uniquely gifted humans with imagination, isn't it a bit backwards to assume that imagination is a hindrance to hearing God's voice? Isn't it more likely that imagination is an important medium for hearing God's voice?[33]

3. Jesus tells us in John 10:4 that the sheep follow the Master because they know his voice. How easy is it for you to recognize the voice of Jesus? When you hear it, how easy is it for you to then follow him where he's leading?

4. Psalm 143:10 reminds us that God desires to teach us his will—through the Spirit. What do you think it means for the Holy Spirit to lead us "on level ground"?

> The gifts of the Spirit are not techniques. They're gifts. A gift isn't something you master—it's something you receive. So if you want an increase in the gift of prophecy, ask God for it in prayer. And be specific. Tell God not only what but also why and how. Why do you want an increase in the gift of prophecy? How will you use it when he gives it to you? When we ask specifically, our eager desire is refined by the way of love. Our motives get picked apart. Our ego gets weeded out. We are made into mature recipients to use the power of the Spirit's gifts. Prophecy is a gift for the building up of the church because prophecy surrenders to love. . . . So ask, and ask specifically, so that God can refine your desire by love, entrusting powerful gifts to mature vessels.[34]

5. Learning to hear the Shepherd's voice and then speaking it in love requires risk and obedience. Where do you fall on the following scale when it comes to risking and obeying? (There's no pressure to be a certain ranking—just circle where you currently are.)

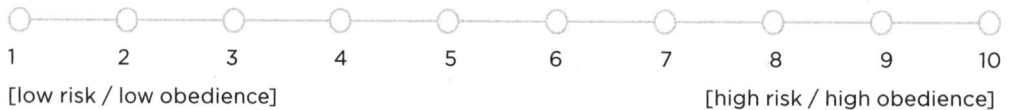

```
O----O----O----O----O----O----O----O----O----O
1    2    3    4    5    6    7    8    9    10
```

[low risk / low obedience]   [high risk / high obedience]

Consider, with no shame or ego, why you ranked yourself where you did. Where would you like to be . . . and what's one step you could make toward that goal?

STUDY 2

THE PURPOSE OF PROPHECY

Imagine meeting someone at a large social gathering. As you try to get to know her, you quickly notice that—no matter what question is being asked—she always brings the conversation back to one point . . . that she's a pilot. You mention your son is traveling home next week, and she lets you know she never flies commercial because she owns a plane. Someone else in the group reveals his fear of heights, and she shares about the highest she's ever flown. If the topic changes to weather conditions . . . well, you get the picture.

All her conversations eventually lead back to one thing. The same is true with prophecy. But unlike the topic of flying, the topic of prophecy is actually grounding. That's because all prophecy directs us toward Jesus.

Old Testament prophecy leads us *to* Jesus. In Luke 24:44, Jesus said, "This is what I told you while I was still with you: Everything must be fulfilled that is written about me in the Law of Moses, the Prophets and the Psalms."

New Testament prophecy leads us *along* with Jesus, the ultimate, embodied revelation of God's heart. We see this in Revelation 19:10 when John, while caught up in his vision, encounters an angel around the throne of God who proclaims "the Spirit of prophecy who bears testimony to Jesus."

The spiritual gift of prophecy is God using a human voice to show people his character. It's one thing to be told that Jesus weeps as you weep (see John 11:35), that he can empathize with your weakness (see Hebrews 4:15), that he enters into your pain (see Matthew 8:17). That's comforting. It's quite another to discover he saw you and wept beside you while you crafted a note explaining why your life wasn't worth living—and to be told in the most direct way possible that God has numbered your days, they're not up yet, and this isn't the end of your story. That is the power of prophecy—Jesus as generally revealed on the pages of Scripture is personally revealed to us in the midst of today's circumstances.

Read: Luke 24:44; Revelation 19:10; Hebrews 4:15

1. *All prophecy directs us to Jesus.* Did you already know this, or did you think that many of the Bible's prophecies were simply about various unrelated future events? How does seeing them all connect to Jesus help your faith?

2. What most stands out to you about Jesus' words in Luke 24:44? Why?

Some confuse biblical prophecy with future-telling or divinely informed prediction, and occasionally Scripture, particularly in the Old Testament, does have examples of this. But that is not the primary function of the prophetic. "Prophecy does not mean, in the first instance, 'to predict,'" writes author and priest Thomas Green, "but rather to speak on behalf of another."[35] When we understand prophecy as prediction, we are focusing on a peripheral feature of the prophetic, not its primary focus. . . . Through prophecy (among other means), the Holy Spirit pushes the teachings of Jesus from the head, where they can be remembered, down into the heart, where they can heal and become a new foundation for us to live from. Prophecy personally reveals who God is in a way that plunges through the intellect right down to a revelation in the heart.[36]

3. We see the continual thread of prophecy about Jesus that began in Genesis continuing in Revelation 19:10. What stands out to you the most in this verse about worship, the Spirit of prophecy, and the testimony of Jesus?

4. What does Hebrews 4:15 reveal about Jesus' ability to empathize with us? How might that truth be made even more personal through a prophetic word shared with a person going through a particular crisis?

One of the ways we grow in prophecy is by fostering the closely related spiritual practice of encouragement. Prophecy involves speaking about things beyond our normal awareness or ability to observe by the Spirit's revelation, while encouragement is based on information available to us through normal observation. In other words, encouragement is prophecy by what you can see, and prophecy is encouragement by what only God can see. . . . When you encourage someone, you're not just being nice; you're being like God. You're acting in harmony with his Spirit. . . . So if you desire prophecy, make a commitment to become a person of encouragement.[37]

5. To *encourage* literally means to "put courage" into others by noticing their actions and then helping them to keep expressing that part of themselves. Who are three people you can encourage this week? What specific "courage" do you want to put into them?

Person's name	How you will encourage (put courage into) that person
1.	
2.	
3.	

STUDY 3

WHAT WE EAGERLY DESIRE

Most people, when it comes to their all-time favorite band, aren't just fans but *fanatics*. They don't just find the songs catchy; they connect with them on a deeper level. So what happens when that band—which, by the way, hasn't toured in years—announces they're going on tour? Will those fans wait to see if the band is coming to their city? Will they wait until the day of the concert to see if tickets are available?

No way. They're camping out days before the tickets go on sale. (They didn't name their pet bulldog after the lead singer for nothing.) They don't casually desire to be part of the experience. They eagerly desire to experience every bit of it. They are all in!

Now imagine that passion on an exponentially higher level and you will get a taste of what Paul means when he urges believers to eagerly desire the gifts of the Spirit: "Follow the way of love and eagerly desire gifts of the Spirit, especially prophecy" (1 Corinthians 14:1). The English word *eagerly* is a translation of the Greek *zeloo*, which "literally means to 'covet' or 'burn with zeal' for a person or a thing."[38] It's a term Paul uses three times in 1 Corinthians "to describe the attitude we should have toward spiritual gifts."[39]

Some of us relate to God's voice passively: *If God wants to speak to me, I'm right here.* Behind that posture is often a fear of manufacturing an experience that's less than authentic. And there's some wisdom in that feeling. We don't want to get swept up in emotion or hype or perform psychological tricks on our minds. But to relate to God's voice passively is also to completely ignore the straightforward teaching of Scripture (see Revelation 3:15–16). We should think constantly about God's whisper, look for every inkling that he's speaking to us, and soak up every word from his lips like it's the most exciting news we can imagine.

Having eager desire is the opposite of being passive. It's being active. And it's being all in with Jesus (see 1 John 2:6).

Read: 1 Corinthians 14:1; Revelation 3:15–16; 1 John 2:6

1. What is something in your everyday life you constantly think about and eagerly desire? Do you have the same eager desire when it comes to the gift of prophecy? Why or why not?

2. In 1 Corinthians 14:1, Paul writes that you should "eagerly desire" the gift of prophecy, but you are also to "follow the way of love." Why is love is an essential part of prophecy?

God eagerly desires to pass redemption through one ordinary human vessel to another, so we should eagerly desire to hear his voice. God doesn't want a team with a few star players. He wants everyone to play. If we really believed that, we'd eagerly desire prophecy. If we really grasped that God is generous and abundant, tenacious in His pursuit of people but equally stubborn and insistent on bringing that redemption through the likes of us, maybe instead of telling God, "I'm here if you want to say anything," we'd ask, "God, what are you saying today? Is there something you want to say to someone else through me?"[40]

3. Why do you think people often react passively to God's voice? What does Revelation 3:15–16 say about the dangers of being spiritually lukewarm?

4. What does being all in with Jesus look like according to 1 John 2:6? How can you be more active in your eagerness to experience the gift of prophecy?

As you learn to listen for God's voice, it's important to know that there are three aspects to every prophetic utterance: revelation, interpretation, and application. *Revelation* refers to the thought, image, or insight delivered to the listener by the Holy Spirit. . . . *Interpretation* is the process of deciphering divine intent and meaning from revelation. When you hear a word or see a picture, the next step is to ask, "Lord, what are you saying through this word or picture?" . . . *Application* is the final step. After receiving a revelation and deciphering the interpretation, ask, "What should I do with it?" Is this prophetic insight meant to be shared with an individual, offered to a community or group, prayed into being without sharing aloud, or something else?[41]

5. Which of the three steps of listening for God's voice (revelation, interpretation, or application) do you struggle with the most? Why that particular step?

If you've heard God speak, think back to that specific time. Write down below what you heard, how you interpreted it, and how you acted on it.

Revelation (what you heard)

Interpretation (how you deciphered it)

Application (how you acted on it)

CATCH UP AND READ AHEAD

Connect with a group member this week to talk about some of the insights from this session. Use any of the prompts below to guide your discussion.

- How do you see prophecy today as different from prophecy in the Bible?
- What feeling arises when someone has a prophetic word for you? Why?
- What is the biggest concern you have around the topic of prophecy?
- Is hearing and speaking a message from God part of your church life?
- Is your imagination more helpful or distracting when it comes to prophecy?
- How might the gift of prophecy help you know the Holy Spirit better?

Use this time to complete any of the personal study and reflection questions from previous days that you weren't able to finish. Make a note below of any questions that you've had or significant insights and breakthroughs that you've gained.

Read chapter 9 in *The Familiar Stranger* before the next group session. Use the space below to make note of anything that stands out to you or encourages you.

WEEK 5

BEFORE GROUP MEETING	Read chapter 9 in *The Familiar Stranger* Read the Welcome section (page 76)
GROUP MEETING	Discuss the Connect questions Watch the video teaching for session 5 Discuss the questions that follow as a group Do the closing exercise and pray (pages 76–80)
STUDY 1	Complete the personal study (pages 82–84)
STUDY 2	Complete the personal study (pages 85–87)
STUDY 3	Complete the personal study (pages 88–90)
CATCH UP AND READ AHEAD (BEFORE WEEK 6 GROUP MEETING)	Connect with someone in your group Read chapter 11 in *The Familiar Stranger* Complete any unfinished personal studies (page 91)

HEALING

"When Jesus healed the sick he bore witness to a time when all suffering would cease."

JOHN WIMBER, *KINGDOM COME*[42]

WELCOME | READ ON YOUR OWN

If we're reading the Bible to discover *if* God wants to heal today, we will get a clear, straightforward answer: *He does.* But if we're reading the Bible to discover *how* to join God in healing, we're likely to leave more confused than when we came. Scripture doesn't provide a formula. Yet it also doesn't keep us entirely in the dark.

Healing is both mysterious and miraculous. So perhaps it's good to begin with a definition: *Healing is a sign of the kingdom that points to salvation—the substance of the kingdom.* Healing acts as a sign pointing to the kingdom that's coming. It is not the kingdom itself, nor is it salvation. Healing is a bit like being in the kitchen with the chef and getting an advance taste of batter. It's good, but you know something better is coming!

Unfortunately, for many believers today the topic is divisive. Yet the supernatural healing of the body was a relatively common occurrence in the book of Acts. It's also listed as one of the gifts of the Spirit given to the church in 1 Corinthians 12. The Bible doesn't shy away from or sensationalize healing. It's not extra special, nor is it hush-hush. It's just another ministry of the church—like preaching, wisdom, encouragement, administration, and prophecy.

Healing doesn't need to be controversial, but it is complicated. That's because suffering is real—and suffering hurts. Whether God brings healing or not, our stories of experiencing illness and seeking healing are sure to change us forever. In this session, we'll look at what the Bible teaches about the divine healing of the body, list six key ingredients of healing, and provide a consistent practice for supernatural healing prayer.

CONNECT | 10 MINUTES

Get the session started by choosing one or both of the following questions to discuss together as a group:

- What is something that spoke to you from last week's personal study?

  — or —

- Was there a time when you and others prayed for your (or another's) healing and the results were miraculous? What was that experience like?

WATCH | 25 MINUTES

Now watch the video for this session. Below is an outline of the key points covered during the teaching. Record any key concepts that stand out to you.

OUTLINE

I. The Gift of Healing
A. Healing reflects God's kingdom breaking into the present world.
B. Sin disrupted creation, bringing sickness and suffering into humanity.
C. Healing offers a glimpse of the future restoration promised by God.

II. Healing in the Bible
A. Healing is a recurring theme throughout both Old and New Testaments.
B. Jesus consistently paired healing with proclaiming the kingdom of God.
C. Healing is a normal part of the church's ministry, not an exception.

III. The Complexity of Healing
A. Healing is complicated because suffering is real—and suffering hurts.
B. We live in a tension theologians call the already / not yet.
C. Healing requires spiritual maturity and sensitivity to navigate its challenges.

IV. Ingredients for Healing
A. Faith plays a role in opening hearts to God's healing power.
B. Spiritual preparation, like prayer and fasting, enhances receptivity to healing.
C. Simple, heartfelt prayers are often the most effective when it comes to healing.

V. Healing as a Sign
A. Healing points to the coming kingdom—but it is not the kingdom itself.
B. Healing provides a foretaste of eternal life and complete restoration.
C. The Holy Spirit uses healing to make God's promises tangible and personal.

NOTES

DISCUSS | 35 MINUTES

Discuss what you just watched by answering the following questions.

1. The healing of the body is a *sign*—a preview of the promised future, an aspect of the coming kingdom of God. What does this sign mean to you personally?

2. There are so many amazing stories in the Gospels of healings that Jesus performed. Which story is your favorite? Why that particular story?

3. The raising of Lazarus from the dead as told in John 11 was miraculous, but even he eventually died. How does knowing that all healing is temporary this side of heaven provide believers in Christ with the correct kingdom perspective?

4. When Jesus healed, his prayers were short and simple (see Mark 1:41; Luke 7:14; and Matthew 9:6). Why do you think believers today are often more comfortable with long, eloquent prayers when asking God for the miraculous?

5. Do you believe that you can grow in power when it comes to healing just like you can in other spiritual gifts like teaching, service, and prophecy? If so, what does that imply you must do to grow? If you don't think you can grow in the power to heal, why not?

RESPOND | 10 MINUTES

Healing can happen instantaneously. We see this in many biblical accounts as well as in contemporary examples. But there are times when we pray and don't see immediate results. In those cases, persistence is essential. Consider the story of Jesus and the blind man in Bethsaida:

> They came to Bethsaida, and some people brought a blind man and begged Jesus to touch him. He took the blind man by the hand and led him outside the village. When he had spit on the man's eyes and put his hands on him, Jesus asked, "Do you see anything?" He looked up and said, "I see people; they look like trees walking around." Once more Jesus put his hands on the man's eyes. Then his eyes were opened, his sight was restored, and he saw everything clearly.
>
> MARK 8:22-25

Notice the man's vision at first improved but was not healed. When we pray for healing, we may initially see only slight improvement. If so, we need to keep praying. If Jesus had to do that, we should expect the same.

What stands out to you in the story of Jesus healing the blind man's sight? Why?

When it comes to important issues at home and work, how would you rate your overall level of persistence? Given this, how can you increase your persistence when praying for healing?

PRAY | 10 MINUTES

Ask God to help you know that he desires healing. Commit to leaving the timing and method in his hands. Thank him that your prayers don't need to be long or eloquent to be heard—that you can simply come to him and ask for the gift of healing. Ask for the Lord to help you be persistent in your prayers, for both yourself and others.

PERSONAL STUDY

As you explored during this week's group time, healing isn't limited to Bible stories from the past or reserved for "super-elite" Christians. It is a gift from the Holy Spirit that is available to all believers. This week's personal study will help you further explore the practice of healing prayer, the role faith plays, and how to grow in spiritual power. After the readings, look up the passages indicated and write down your responses to the questions. If you're part of a group, you will be given a few minutes to share your insights at the start of the next session. If you are reading *The Familiar Stranger* alongside this study, first review chapter 9 of the book.

STUDY 1

THE ALREADY AND NOT YET

"Are we there yet?" It's the question kids ask three minutes into the drive of a cross-country trip. As adults, we laugh or roll our eyes. But we do the same when facing high-stakes issues.

We grow impatient when we're stuck in the unknown of a hard situation. Especially when an illness isn't healing but is actually accelerating in the wrong direction. We want a fast pass to hope . . . and healing. How are we to interpret it when we've asked for healing, and we know God can heal us, but nothing changes?

Theologians call this type of spiritual tension the "already / not yet." We live in the *already* right now. Jesus is victorious over sin, and we can know that victory here and now (see 2 Corinthians 5:17). However, we also remain in the *not yet*, because the full experience of that victory is still in the future, awaiting Jesus' return (see Romans 8:18–19).

The final victory is in the future, but the promise is already here: We will be raised with Christ—and raised bodily. Heaven, according to Jesus and the biblical authors, is not an escape. It's a renewal—the renewal of the earth and the renewal of our bodies. When God makes all things new, there will be no more death, crying, or pain (see Revelation 21:4–5).

Over a lifetime of apprenticeship to Jesus, you will experience the overwhelming joy of the *already* and experience the pain of the *not yet*. That tension is made bearable only by the God who didn't shy away from either—the One who sent Jesus to be both a victorious Savior ushering in a new kingdom and "a man of suffering" (Isaiah 53:3).

So buckle up. We're not fully there. But we are already experiencing a taste of where we're headed. And we're closer than ever to the *not yet* of all that awaits.

Read: 2 Corinthians 5:17; Romans 8:18–19; Revelation 21:5

1. Is there a situation in which you or a loved one is in need of healing? If so, how would you describe the joy of the *already* and the pain of the *not yet* playing out simultaneously?

2. In 2 Corinthians 5:17, how does the apostle Paul describe the *already* side of the kingdom that we get to experience now?

> Healing is most often sought in the midst of suffering, so when we seek healing, we're asking God to touch something that's probably already life-defining and make it life-*redefining*. This is the one aspect that, I believe, distinguishes healing from other spiritual gifts. Many people—not all, but many—respond to bad teaching with a yawn. But many people respond to an unmet request for healing by redefining the God they pray to. Some people have a story of healing. Others have a story of suffering. And plenty of us have both. . . . Healing is complicated and requires a community of spiritual maturity and pastoral sensitivity.[43]

3. The pain we experience in the *not yet* can be overwhelming. What does Paul reveal in Romans 8:19 about your present sufferings, coming glory, and creation's eager expectation?

4. Jesus is both our victorious Savior who is ushering in the coming kingdom and a suffering servant. Describe the traits of Jesus in each of these roles.

How is Jesus a victorious Savior?

How is Jesus a suffering servant?

If you're wondering, "Why didn't God heal?" in a particular situation, that's a more complicated question, one without a clean and tidy biblical answer. The safest thing about praying for healing is that the God we pray to is so good that he repurposes everything—everything, even our suffering—into our redemption. God can and will redeem everything you experience in this life if you offer it to him. So yes, healing is complicated, but not as complicated as we tend to make it. To sum up all of that in a single phrase: Healing is an "already" taste of the "not yet" eternal life we still await.[44]

5. Heaven is not an escape but a renewal of the earth and our bodies. How is this described in Revelation 21:5—specifically in relation to our pain and healing?

STUDY 2

COMING ATTRACTIONS

At practically every movie theater, there is something that happens before the main feature begins. After you've purchased your overpriced popcorn and drink and settled into your seat, you are shown a preview of coming attractions. These trailers give you a hint of what's to come. But if you think the trailer tells the entire story, you're wrong. It's not the movie. It's just a *taste* of what's to come. One that's designed to make you long for the actual thing.

The coming attractions are a sign. They are not the movie. In the same way, the healing of the body is a sign—a preview of the promised future, an aspect of the inbreaking kingdom of God you know now in part but one day will know fully (see 1 Corinthians 13:12).

The raising of Lazarus is likely Jesus' most astounding miraculous sign outside of his own resurrection. Healing doesn't get more supernatural than raising the dead. But this account, maybe more than any of the others, holds the healing ministry of Jesus (a sign of the kingdom) in proper context next to the salvation offered in Jesus (the substance of the kingdom). In the resurrection of Lazarus, Jesus was reaching back to a promise made in John 5:25, but he was also reaching forward to his own resurrection. The sign is a miracle pointing to a person.

Jesus says to the grieving, "I am the resurrection and the life" (John 11:25), and then calls Lazarus out of the grave. There is hope *now*—real, embodied hope in our midst. That's the sign. Then Jesus suffers, dies, is put in his own tomb, and walks out three days later. There is hope *forever*—a hope that will never be taken away. That's substance.

Healing is a sign pointing to a kingdom that's coming . . . whether you want it or not and whether you see it or not. It is coming for sure, and coming for good (in both senses of the word *good*—it's for our good, and it's here to stay). But healing is not the kingdom itself. It's not salvation, not the substance. It is only a sign.

Read: 1 Corinthians 13:12; John 5:25, 28–29; John 20:31

1. Why is it important to recognize that healing is a *sign* that points to the kingdom that's coming but not the *substance* of the kingdom itself?

2. Paul writes, "For now we see only a reflection as in a mirror; then we shall see face to face. Now I know in part; then I shall know fully, even as I am fully known" (1 Corinthians 13:12). Do you look forward more to knowing things fully (knowledge) or being fully known (intimacy)? Explain your response.

> "Lazarus, come out," Jesus called from the mouth of the tomb. A command that restored life to the dead body of Lazarus, who emerged in his graveclothes. Jesus called out in a loud voice. That's how he raised Lazarus, according to John 11. Surely the disciples were reminded of what he had said previously: "A time is coming when all who are in their graves will hear his voice and come out—those who have done what is good will rise to live, and those who have done what is evil will rise to be condemned" (John 5:28–29).[45]

3. How was Jesus' resurrection of Lazarus a demonstration of this promise he had made? What point was Jesus making in the moment—and for us today?

4. Read John 20:30–31. Jesus also reached forward to his own resurrection to show that the healing of Lazarus was a sign pointing to the future kingdom.

What two reasons does John give in this passage for why so many of Jesus' signs were recorded?

> Healing is a taste of the batter when a cake is coming. Our posture toward healing should be childlike, filled with wonder, desperate for a taste, wanting it so bad we can't stand it, ready to trade anything for one lick of that batter-coated spoon. But we also need to be absolutely certain that we've got a whole cake coming, absolutely certain that this taste isn't the best thing or the whole thing. This taste is just a preview of what's promised. . . . *Healing is a sign of the Kingdom, so we seek it and ask for it now, hungry for a taste of what's to come.*[46]

5. Think of a current situation in which you are seeking healing. Divide it into two parts—the sign (the real hope now) and the substance (the real hope forever).

The Situation	The Sign (real hope now)	The Substance (real hope forever)

How does seeing the situation in this way reframe your hurt . . . and how does it reframe your healing?

STUDY 3

THE FAITH INGREDIENT

When people see that someone is hurting, they will often encourage that person to have faith that everything will work out okay. It sounds positive and hopeful. It's a popular sentiment in many get-well-quick cards. The problem is that it doesn't really work. Generic faith doesn't do anything specific. It *matters* in who or what we place our faith. Putting our faith in this world, our job, the lottery, the government, or the economy never turns out well.

God alone is worthy of our faith, because he alone is trustworthy and powerful enough to always come through. Everyone and everything else will ultimately fall short. Our faith in God changes everything. As we read in Hebrews 11:6, "Without faith it is impossible to please God, because anyone who comes to him must believe that he exists and that he rewards those who earnestly seek him."

The Bible is clear this kind of faith is an essential ingredient to healing. In Mark 6:5–6, while in the throes of his growing miraculous ministry, Jesus returned to his home-town. We read, "He could not do any miracles there, except lay his hands on a few sick people and heal them. He was amazed at their lack of faith." A few chapters later, we see the other side of the same coin when Jesus heals the blind man Bartimaeus. "'Go,' said Jesus, 'your faith has healed you.' Immediately he received his sight and followed Jesus along the road" (10:52).

While Jesus healed frequently in the Gospels, he didn't provide a single model or step-by-step approach to supernatural healing. There's mystery to the miraculous.

Everyone who acquires a taste for the wondrous kingdom sign of miraculous healing also stomachs plenty of disappointment. This is why we must pray for healing by keeping the sign in proper perspective with the substance—trusting that, while Jesus has not revealed a God we can perfectly understand, he has revealed a God we can perfectly trust.

Read: Hebrews 11:6; Mark 6:5–6; Mark 10:52

1. According to Hebrews 11:6, it is impossible to please God without faith. What are two things we must believe when we come to him in faith?

2. It takes a lot to amaze Jesus. What, according to Mark 6:5–6, amazed Jesus about his hometown? What was the outcome of this spiritual condition?

A quick word of caution: shame or condemnation can come in if we think, *God would've healed that person, but I didn't have enough faith.* . . . Faith is one of the ingredients to healing, yet there are other factors, and there's a lot of mystery. You can be confident of this: God wants to heal. Faith plays a part in healing. And God is merciful and gracious, slow to anger, and abounding in steadfast love (see Exodus 34:6), so if you feel shame or condemnation, that's not God condemning you; it's the deceiver. Throw it out.[47]

3. Have you ever felt shame or condemnation because you felt you didn't have enough faith for a prayer of healing to work? How does the fact that "God is merciful and gracious" reassure you that it isn't God who is condemning you?

4. In Mark 10:52, Jesus healed the blind man's sight instantaneously—though healing doesn't always happen this fast. Have you ever experienced a moment of immediate healing? If so, how did it come about?

> Jesus was a miraculous healer, but by far his most effective act of healing came by suffering and ultimately dying on a cross. The Bible, which is peppered cover to cover with miraculous healing, is also peppered cover to cover with redemptive suffering. . . . Jesus has not revealed a God with satisfying answers to our individual stories and questions, but he has provided a God who suffered and suffers alongside us, is personally acquainted with the cost of suffering, and has emphatically promised to never let a drop of my suffering or yours go to waste.[48]

5. Consider this truth that the Bible is filled with stories of miraculous healings but also with stories of redemptive suffering. Record your experience in both realms.

> Experience with miraculous healings:

> Experience with redemptive suffering:

What are some of the ways that has God used these times of healing and suffering to draw you closer to him?

CATCH UP AND READ AHEAD

Connect with a group member this week to talk about some of the insights from this session. Use any of the prompts below to guide your discussion.

- How has this session changed or challenged your views on healing?
- Why do you think the topic of healing is so divisive among Christians?
- In what ways do you personally struggle with this topic?
- What role do you think your faith plays in healing?
- When praying for a person to be healed, does it feel more risky or holy?
- What is the biggest question you want to ask God about healing?

Use this time to complete any of the personal study and reflection questions from previous days that you weren't able to finish. Make a note below of any questions that you've had or significant insights and breakthroughs that you've gained.

Read chapter 11 in *The Familiar Stranger* before the next group session. Use the space below to make note of anything that stands out to you or encourages you.

WEEK 6

BEFORE GROUP MEETING	Read chapter 11 in *The Familiar Stranger* Read the Welcome section (page 94)
GROUP MEETING	Discuss the Connect questions Watch the video teaching for session 6 Discuss the questions that follow as a group Do the closing exercise and pray (pages 94–98)
STUDY 1	Complete the personal study (pages 100–102)
STUDY 2	Complete the personal study (pages 103–105)
STUDY 3	Complete the personal study (pages 106–108)
WRAP IT UP	Connect with someone in your group (page 109) Complete any unfinished personal studies Connect with your group about the next study you want to go through together

REDEMPTIVE SUFFERING

*"There are many things that can only be
seen through eyes that have cried."*

HAROLD S. KUSHNER, *WHEN BAD THINGS HAPPEN
TO GOOD PEOPLE* [49]

WELCOME | READ ON YOUR OWN

The sad truth is that the experience of suffering is common to every human life. Yet while suffering is common to all people, it is also unique to each person. Everyone in history has suffered, but no one has ever suffered in exactly the same way.

The most natural human response to the inconvenient truth of suffering is to do our best to avoid it and minimize its effects when it intrudes into our lives. Given this, it is striking how the biblical narrative takes a decidedly alternative view on suffering . . . a redemptive view. It reveals that God did not create a world of pain but a paradise that he called "good." This very good creation was corrupted by the deceiver. But the story doesn't end there. While Satan is the author of suffering, Jesus is the redeemer of suffering.

Perhaps the best-kept secret about the Holy Spirit is that his power is just as living, active, and present in our suffering as it is in our triumphs. All the pain we face is repurposed by the Spirit as a key ingredient in the redemption of the world.

In this final session, we will bring these ideas from the cloudy place of theology and ground them in the reality of our daily lives. We will do this by looking at how God redeems the pain he doesn't remove; how the power of the Spirit in Jesus' suffering is in our own; how we to choose what our suffering does to us; and how we can discover the process by which the Spirit converts surrendered suffering into love, compassion, gratitude, groaning, and redemption.

God doesn't merely grieve or offer sympathy for our suffering from a safe distance. He enters into it and invites us to join him there.

CONNECT | 10 MINUTES

Get the session started by choosing one or both of the following questions to discuss together as a group:

- What is something that spoke to you from last week's personal study?

  — or —

- Do you tend to grow closer to or further from God in times of suffering? Why is that your tendency—and what is the result?

WATCH | 25 MINUTES

Now watch the video for this session. Below is an outline of the key points covered during the teaching. Record any key concepts that stand out to you.

OUTLINE

I. The Reality of Suffering
A. The sad truth is that the experience of suffering is common to every human.
B. However, while suffering is common to all, it is also unique to each individual.
C. Avoiding or minimizing suffering is a natural but incomplete response.

II. God's Role in Suffering
A. God did not create a world of pain but a paradise he called "good."
B. Satan is the author of suffering. Jesus is the redeemer of suffering.
C. Jesus made suffering "sufferable" because he dealt with suffering by suffering.

III. The Transformative Power of Suffering
A. Suffering exposes weakness, creating opportunities for love and connection.
B. Suffering fosters compassion by helping us empathize with others' pain.
C. Suffering endured thoughtfully instills gratitude for the things that truly matter and satisfy.

IV. The Holy Spirit's Work in Suffering
A. The Holy Spirit works with both the good and the bad in our lives for renewal.
B. The Holy Spirit repurposes the atrocity of suffering into the creative force of glory.
C. Those filled with the Holy Spirit are "pregnant" with this world's renewal.

V. Responding to Suffering
A. God doesn't promise to protect us from pain but promises to redeem every moment of pain.
B. Lament begins with taking stock of the gap between our present and God's promised future.
C. Our response determines whether suffering will diminish or refine us.

NOTES

DISCUSS | 35 MINUTES

Discuss what you just watched by answering the following questions.

1. Suffering is common to every human. Though you may not often talk about it, how has pain and illness played a part of your or your family's story?

2. Paul writes, "We also glory in our sufferings, because we know that suffering produces perseverance; perseverance, character; and character, hope" (Romans 5:3–4). How is it possible for something glorious to come from suffering? How have you experienced this?

3. Suffering exposes weakness. Is it hard for you to admit you need help and accept the love of others when you're sick or recovering from an illness? Why or why not?

4. An unexpected diagnosis can suddenly reveal how the things we take for granted are actually life's greatest treasures. What do you most value in your life? How might you become more present in those areas you most value?

5. Why is it important to remember that Jesus is not only our Savior but also our suffering Redeemer (see Hebrews 9:12)? How does Jesus make your suffering sufferable?

RESPOND | 10 MINUTES

Lament is the practice of groaning with the Spirit in the midst of suffering. It is most frequently encompassed in the repeated biblical phrase, "How long, Lord?" (Psalm 13:1). Sadly, lament is mostly absent in the modern church. The consequence is that many of us do not know how to talk to God in the wake of suffering, leading to silence in the very circumstances the Holy Spirit and God's holy people historically grew loudest in their groans. As Paul writes:

> In the same way, the Spirit helps us in our weakness. We do not know what we ought to pray for, but the Spirit himself intercedes for us through wordless groans. And he who searches our hearts knows the mind of the Spirit, because the Spirit intercedes for God's people in accordance with the will of God.
>
> ROMANS 8:26–27

The groans of the Holy Spirit within us are laments *with hope*. Because we have a Redeemer who keeps his promises, we can grieve, wail, and groan in the in-between—but we do all of it with hope.

How do you think the loss of practicing lament in the church has caused believers to forget how to talk to God in the wake of suffering?

What does Paul reveal in Romans 8:26–27 about how the Holy Spirit helps you in your groanings when you don't know what to say or pray?

PRAY | 10 MINUTES

As you close this study, pray for the assurance to know God is *with* you in suffering, enters *into* your suffering, and walks *alongside* you in your suffering. Pray that God will redeem your pain and weave it into his greater story of restoration and glory. Ask for a heart that is softened by your own suffering—a heart that enables you to empathize and co-suffer with others in their pain.

PERSONAL STUDY

The focus of this final session is on what it means to experience redemptive suffering. During the group time, you looked at the reality of suffering, God's role in suffering, the transformative power of suffering, the Holy Spirit's work in suffering, and how to respond to suffering. This final personal study is designed to take you—through stories and Scripture—deeper into these topics on redemptive suffering. After the readings, look up the passages indicated and write down your responses to the questions. If you are reading *The Familiar Stranger* alongside this study, first review chapter 11 of the book.

STUDY 1

HOW GOD FEELS ABOUT SUFFERING

We are curious creatures. We look around and ask why things are the way they are. *Why do we park in driveways and drive on parkways? Why do we sink slowly in quicksand? Why do offers with no strings attached always have strings?*

Then there are the big questions—the ones that keep us up at night and cause us to question our faith. Questions such as, *Why is there suffering?* As we've seen in this session, Satan is the author of suffering, not God. But that leads to an important question that colors and shapes the previous one: *How does God feel about suffering?*

The answer is found in Genesis 6:5–6: "The Lord saw how great the wickedness of the human race had become on the earth, and that every inclination of the thoughts of the human heart was only evil all the time. The Lord regretted that he had made human beings on the earth, and his heart was deeply troubled."

God looked at the consequences of sin and "regretted" making creation in the first place. God's elation in Genesis 1 is matched by his grief in Genesis 6. So, how does God feel about suffering? It grieves his heart—even more than it grieves our own.

No wonder, then, that God's presence and power are especially focused on those who suffer—the poor, the oppressed, the marginalized. As Jesus said, "When you give a banquet, invite the poor, the crippled, the lame, the blind, and you will be blessed. Although they cannot repay you, you will be repaid at the resurrection of the righteous" (Luke 14:13–14).

God is our Father, and every loving parent is quick to give care to a child in crisis. God is a parent whose heart is disproportionately drawn to the suffering child. Why does this matter? Because God doesn't merely grieve or offer sympathy for our suffering from a safe distance. He enters into it. Jesus is the redeemer of our suffering.

Read: Genesis 1:31; Genesis 6:5–6; Luke 14:13–14

1. We all know how *we* feel about suffering, but have you ever wondered how *God* feels about it? Why is that important and why does it matter so much?

2. God goes from elation over creation in Genesis 1:31 (pronouncing it "very good") to being deeply troubled over humanity in Genesis 6:5–6. What led to this shift?

> The biblical story does not begin with conflict but union. . . . God did not create a world of pain but a place he called "good" every step of the way and "very good" when his work was done. He created people to live in paradise, the union of heaven and earth, apart from death, grief, sadness, and pain. Turn just a single page, though, and God's very good creation was corrupted by a deceiver. God told one story. The serpent told another. Humanity believed the serpent, and the world as we know it is the product of the lie our ancestors believed. As my friend Pete Hughes often says, "The story you live in is the story you live out." All of our trouble is the product of a curse that infected every aspect of God's good world.[50]

3. Reflect on the idea that the biblical story doesn't begin with conflict but union. Why is this important to remember—especially when it comes to questions about suffering and pain?

4. "The story you live *in* is the story you live *out*." What story would you say you're living *in* regarding suffering? More importantly, how are you living it *out*?

> Story I am living in (my situation with suffering):

> How I am living out that story (my choices within suffering):

> Why would a life begin in a mother's womb only to die there before he or she lives a single day? Why does a tsunami wave wash over the coast of Indonesia or a hurricane ram into the heart of New Orleans? Why does a disease in one person in Wuhan spread until the whole world is paralyzed? Not because God willed any of it but because the consequences of this curse are of the furthest-reaching variety. Please don't misunderstand. This isn't saying that all suffering is the direct result of any individual's particular sin. The point is that living outside of Eden has consequences. Death and sin have infected the very world we live in, and all suffering is a symptom of sin (the world we chose), not God (the good world he created).[51]

5. Jesus said, "When you give a banquet, invite the poor, the crippled, the lame, the blind, and you will be blessed. Although they cannot repay you, you will be repaid at the resurrection of the righteous" (Luke 14:13–14). What do these words reveal about the heart of Jesus toward those who suffer?

STUDY 2

LOVE IN WEAKNESS

We don't just look up to people of great strength. We want to *be* them. When we watch an adventure movie, we don't imagine ourselves as the one being rescued. We're the one doing the rescuing. We dread being seen as weak. And there's nothing like suffering to expose our weakness and fragility. But hiding it only diminishes our chance to love others and to be loved in our weakness. So, what are we to do?

Jesus shows us the answer with his life—loving well in strength *and* in weakness. (By "weakness," we mean that Jesus' supernatural activity was replaced by a willed passivity.)[52] For three years, his disciples knew him as always active, always doing. But in his final twenty-four hours, he was arrested, questioned, whipped, and mocked. He was helped in carrying his cross. He was nailed down to it. Jesus, a beacon of loving strength for three years, now offered that same love in his weakness. He showed not only his *triumphant* weakness on the cross but also his *suffering* weakness in the journey to the cross—and in this way made space for love.

Had Jesus not shown this weakness in Gethsemane, Peter, James, and John would not have been invited to pray with him (see Matthew 26:36–38). It was Jesus' prolonged weakness that afforded his mother, Mary, the opportunity to hear her son's concern when he asked John to care for her (see John 19:26–27). Jesus' weakness is an offering of love to others and, equally, offers space for others to love him in a way they could not love him in his strength.

When Paul experienced a tormenting pain from the enemy, he pleaded with God three times to take it away. God's answer? "My grace is sufficient for you, for my power is made perfect in weakness." And Paul's humble response? "I will boast all the more gladly about my weaknesses, so that Christ's power may rest on me" (2 Corinthians 12:9–10).

There is faith, hope, and love. "But the greatest of these is love" (1 Corinthians 13:13). In our suffering, God shows us how to love in weakness.

Read: Matthew 26:36–38; 1 Corinthians 13:13; 2 Corinthians 12:7–10

1. On a scale of 1 to 10, with 1 being "not much" and 10 being "a lot," how much do you dread showing weakness?

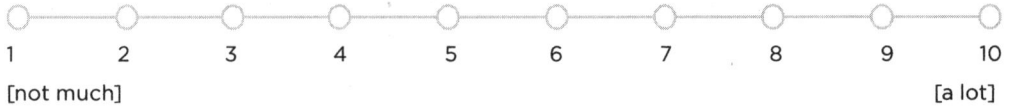

1	2	3	4	5	6	7	8	9	10
[not much]									[a lot]

Based on your rating, how does suffering affect you when it's impossible to hide your need for help?

2. Jesus was a beacon of loving strength for three years—and then, in his final hours, he offered that same love in his weakness. How did Peter, James, and John experience this aspect of Jesus in Gethsemane (see Matthew 26:36–38)?

> Paul tells us that "hope does not put us to shame, because God's love has been poured out into our hearts through the Holy Spirit, who has been given to us" (Romans 5:5). This oft-referenced and deeply true expression of the Spirit's power is nearly always taken on its own, but it's worth remembering that, when Paul wrote it, he framed this Spirit-empowered outpouring of love in the context of our suffering. Suffering exposes our weakness—the very weakness we can offer to others in love and through which we can receive love. The ways God pours his love into our hearts through the Holy Spirit are as beautiful and varied as the turning of a kaleidoscope. But nowhere does the Spirit meet us more profoundly with the experiential, transformational love of God than in the weakness exposed by suffering.[53]

3. Consider the statement, "Suffering exposes our weakness—the very weakness we can offer to others in love and through which we can receive love." How do you respond to this idea? How have you offered your weakness to others and received love through it?

4. Read 2 Corinthians 12:7–10. Even though Paul wanted to be free from his suffering, he also gladly boasted about—even delighted in—his weakness. Why does he say he is able to do this? What does he say is the result of being weak for Christ's sake?

> The most scandalous part of Jesus to ancient ears was that he, the Lord, would suffer. God on a throne? Sure. A God who bleeds? A God who weeps? A God who grieves? Unthinkable. It's understandable why it's such a shock that God would suffer, but consider this. A God who doesn't suffer probably isn't a God worth trusting. Without the courage to crawl down into this world and feel the darkness with the same helplessness as the rest of us, how could God be trusted? How could he be relatable? Without suffering, how could God tell a story deep enough to hold our own suffering?[54]

5. When you are suffering, there's nothing like faith, hope, and love to help make it bearable. Why do you think the *greatest* of these is love (see 1 Corinthians 13:13)? How have you experienced this in a moment of weakness—or in loving someone in that situation?

STUDY 3

SPIRIT-POWERED SUFFERING

The Holy Spirit is our Advocate. The Holy Spirit is our Counselor. And the Holy Spirit is our Comforter. These royal titles bring us great comfort. Especially since it's the Holy Spirit personally advocating, counseling, and comforting us. But what role does the Holy Spirit have in Jesus' suffering . . . as well as our own?

Let's begin with Jesus. At every moment in the story of God incarnate, it is the Holy Spirit who dignifies Jesus' suffering. He makes his suffering substitutionary and repurposes that suffering powerfully for the redemption of all creation. Think about it. Who drove Jesus into the wilderness to be tempted—to resist the very temptations that each of us fail to resist, which is the source of all this suffering in the first place? The Holy Spirit (see Mark 1:12-13). Who enlivened Jesus' body with a resurrection life that not even the cruelty of crucifixion could overcome? The Holy Spirit (see Romans 8:11).

Throughout Jesus' ministry, he promised that same Spirit to us—with increasing frequency the nearer he got to the pinnacle of his suffering. Jesus told his followers, "If you love me, keep my commands. And I will ask the Father, and he will give you another advocate to help you and be with you forever—the Spirit of truth" (see John 14:15-17).

The Spirit is the Comforter present with us in our suffering. The Spirit is the Advocate redeeming our suffering. The Spirit is the Counselor guiding us through the processing and healing of our wounds. The Spirit enables us to continue the cruciform ministry of Jesus, suffering in love on behalf of others. We are given the Spirit to make us suffering redeemers like Jesus. We are filled with the Holy Spirit to make our suffering redemptive, even glorious.

Suffering is connected to glory because suffering—like nothing else in this life—affords us the opportunity to become like Jesus in this chaotic and corrupted world. That's how the Holy Spirit empowers us in our suffering!

Read: Mark 1:12-13; Romans 8:11; John 14:15-17

1. Did you realize that it was the Holy Spirit who led Jesus, immediately after his baptism, into the wilderness to be tempted (see Mark 1:12–13)? What is the significance of these two events happening so close together . . . and in the order they did?

2. Paul wrote, "If the Spirit of him who raised Jesus from the dead is living in you, he who raised Christ from the dead will also give life to your mortal bodies because of his Spirit who lives in you" (Romans 8:11). What does this say about the power of the Holy Spirit in our suffering?

> How does suffering produce glory when we're not reading it on a page but experiencing it in real life? A diagnosis, a loss, an interruption, a betrayal—how is any of that connected to glory? There's nothing intrinsically noble about suffering. Sometimes pain just hurts, suffering is just sad, and grief just has to be gotten through. Sentimentalizing the bad in our lives doesn't make it good. It's still bad, plain and simple. But the Holy Spirit works with both the good and bad in our lives for renewal, so let's wring out the ways—as far as we can define them—that the Holy Spirit not only dignifies our experience but repurposes the atrocity of suffering into the creative force of redemption.[55]

3. Sometimes "pain just hurts, suffering is just sad, and grief just has to be gotten through." How have you found this statement to be true in your experience?

4. The Spirit is our Comforter present in our suffering. The Spirit is our Advocate redeeming our suffering. The Spirit is our Counselor guiding us through the processing and healing of our wounds. In the table below, give an example of how you've personally experienced the Holy Spirit in these three roles.

Comforter	Advocate	Counselor

The Holy Spirit is present and powerful not just in miraculous interventions or mountaintop moments. He can be heard groaning in shocked hospital rooms and overcrowded orphanages, in the tearing open of an eviction notice, in the reading of a suicide note. Yes, the power of the Holy Spirit sounds like the gasps of wonder as Lazarus emerges from his tomb. But the power of the same Spirit is heard also in the wails, sobs, and righteous anger erupting from the grieving, asking for it all to come to an end, for all to be made right, for the full redemption promised by King Jesus.[56]

5. Jesus promised us the same Spirit that was with him (see John 14:15–17)—not just in the mountaintop moments but in everything we do and everywhere we go. As you conclude this study, what do you most want to thank the Holy Spirit for or ask for his help in?

WRAP IT UP

Connect with a group member this week to talk about some of the insights from this session. Use any of the prompts below to guide your discussion.

- In what ways do the words *redemptive suffering* belong together?
- When you experience suffering, what tends to be your first reaction? Why?
- Why do you think God doesn't always remove suffering?
- How can both healing and suffering can be redemptive?
- What does the idea of "surrendered suffering" mean to you?
- How has this study most changed your relationship with the Holy Spirit?

Use this time to go back and complete any of the personal study and reflection questions from previous days that you weren't able to finish. Make a note of what God has revealed to you. Finally, talk with your group about what study you may want to go through next. Put a date on the calendar for when you'll meet next to study God's Word and dive deeper into community.

LEADER'S GUIDE

Thank you for leading your group through this study! What you have chosen to do is valuable and will make a difference in their lives. *The Familiar Stranger* is a six-session study built around video content and small-group interaction. As the group leader, imagine yourself as the host of a party. Your job is to take care of your guests by managing the details so that when your guests arrive, they can focus on one another and on the interaction around the topic for that session.

Your role as the group leader is not to answer all the questions or to reteach the content—the video, book, and study guide will do most of that work. Rather, your job is to guide the experience and cultivate your small group into a connected and engaged community. This will make it a place for your group members to process, question, and reflect on all that they have learned. There are several elements in this leader's guide that will help you as you structure your study and reflection time, so be sure to follow along and take advantage of each one.

BEFORE YOU BEGIN

Before your first meeting, make sure the group members have a copy of this study guide. Alternately, you can hand out the study guides at your first meeting and give the members some time to look over the material and ask any preliminary questions. Also, make sure that the group members are aware they have access to the streaming videos at any time by following the instructions provided with this guide. During your first meeting, ask the members to provide their names, phone numbers, and email addresses so that you can keep in touch.

Generally, the ideal size for a group is eight to ten people, which will ensure that everyone has enough time to participate in discussions. If you have more people, you might want to break up the main group into smaller subgroups. Encourage those who show up at the first meeting to commit to attending the duration of the study, as this will help the group members get to know one another, create stability for the group, and help you know how best to prepare to lead the participants through the material.

Each session begins with an opening reflection in the Welcome section. The questions that follow in the Connect section serve as icebreakers to get the group members thinking about the topic. In the rest of the study, it is generally not a good idea to have everyone answer every question—a free-flowing discussion is more desirable. But with the icebreaker questions, you can go around the circle and ask each person to respond. Encourage shy people to share, but don't force them.

At your first meeting, let the group members know each session contains a personal study section they can use to continue to engage with the content until the next meeting. This section will help cement the concepts presented during the group study time so they can better apply what they have learned about the Holy Spirit.

Let them know that if they choose to do so, they can watch the video for the next session by accessing the streaming code provided with this study guide. Invite them to bring any questions and insights to your next meeting, especially if they had a breakthrough moment or didn't understand something.

PREPARATION FOR EACH SESSION

As the leader, there are a few things you should do to prepare for each meeting:

- **Read through the session.** This will help you become more familiar with the content and know how to structure the discussion times.
- **Decide how the videos will be used.** Determine whether you want the members to watch the videos ahead of time (again, via the streaming access code provided with this study guide) or together as a group.
- **Decide which questions you want to discuss.** Based on the length of your group discussions, you may not be able to get through all the questions. Look over the discussion questions provided in each session and mark which ones you definitely want to cover.
- **Be familiar with the questions you want to discuss.** When the group meets, you will be watching the clock, so make sure you are familiar with the questions you have selected.
- **Pray for your group.** Pray for your group members and ask God to lead them as they study his Word and listen to the Holy Spirit.

In many cases, there will be no one "right" answer to the questions. Answers will vary, especially when the group members are sharing their personal experiences.

STRUCTURING THE DISCUSSION TIME

You will need to determine with your group how long you want your meetings to last so that you can plan your time accordingly. Suggested times for each section have been provided in this study guide, and if you adhere to these times, your group will meet for ninety minutes. However, many groups like to meet for two hours. If this describes your particular group, follow the times listed in the right-hand column of the chart given below.

Section	90 Minutes	120 Minutes
CONNECT (discuss one or more of the opening questions for the session)	10 minutes	20 minutes
WATCH (watch the teaching material together and take notes)	25 minutes	20 minutes
DISCUSS (discuss the study questions you selected ahead of time)	35 minutes	50 minutes
RESPOND (write down key takeaways)	10 minutes	15 minutes
PRAY (pray together and dismiss)	10 minutes	15 minutes

As the group leader, it is up to you to keep track of the time and to keep things on schedule. You might want to set a timer for each segment so that both you and the group members know when the time is up. (There are some good phone apps with timers that play a gentle chime or other pleasant sound instead of a disruptive noise.)

Don't be concerned if group members are less talkative or slow to share. People are often quiet when they are pulling together their ideas, and this might be a new experience for some of them. Just ask a question and let it hang in the air until someone shares. You can then say, "Thank you. What about others? What came to you when you watched that portion of the teaching?"

GROUP DYNAMICS

Leading a group through *The Familiar Stranger* will be rewarding both to you and your members. But you still may encounter challenges along the way! Discussions can get off track. Group members may not be sensitive to the needs and ideas of others. Some might worry that they will be expected to talk about matters that make them feel awkward. Others may express comments that result in disagreements.

To help ease this strain on you and the group, consider the following ground rules:

- When someone raises a question or comment that is off the main topic, suggest you deal with it another time, or, if you feel led to go in that direction, let the group know that you will be spending some time discussing it.

- If someone asks a question that you don't know how to answer, admit it and move on. At your discretion, feel free to invite group members to comment on questions that call for personal experience.

- If you find that one or two people are dominating the discussion time, direct a few questions to others in the group. Outside the main group time, ask the more dominating members to help you draw out the quieter ones. Work to make them part of the solution instead of part of the problem.

- When a disagreement occurs, encourage the group members to process the matter in love. Encourage those on opposite sides to restate what they heard the other side say about the matter, and then invite each side to evaluate if that perception is accurate. Lead the group in examining other passages related to the topic and look for common ground.

When any of these issues arise, encourage your group members to follow these words from Scripture: "Love one another" (John 13:34); "If possible, so far as it depends on you, live at peace with everyone" (Romans 12:18); "Whatever is true . . . noble . . . right . . . pure . . . lovely . . . admirable . . . if anything is excellent or praiseworthy—think about such things" (Philippians 4:8); and, "Everyone should be quick to listen, slow to speak and slow to become angry" (James 1:19). This will make your group time more rewarding and beneficial for everyone who attends.

Thank you for taking the time to lead your group. You are making a difference in your members' lives and having an impact on their (re)introduction the Holy Spirit.

NOTES

1. Eugene H. Peterson, *The Pastor: A Memoir* (HarperOne, 2012).
2. Ligonier Ministries, "The State of Theology," https://thestateoftheology.com/, quoted in Stefani McDade, "Top 5 Heresies Among American Evangelicals," *Christianity Today*, September 19, 2022, https://www.christianitytoday.com/ct/2022/september-web-only/state-of-theology-evangelical-heresy-report-ligonier-survey.html.
3. Simon Ponsonby, *More: How You Can Have More of the Spirit When You Already Have Everything in Christ* (David C. Cook, 2010), 29.
4. Billy Graham, "How to Be Filled with the Spirit," sermon, Greater Los Angeles Crusade, 1949.
5. Strong's Hebrew, "7307.ruach," Bible Hub, accessed June 20, 2024, https://biblehub.com/hebrew/7307.htm; Strong's Greek, "4151.pneuma," Bible Hub, accessed June 20, 2024, https://biblehub.com/greek/4151.htm.
6. Tyler Staton, *The Familiar Stranger: (Re)introducing the Holy Spirit to Those in Search of an Experiential Spirituality* (Nelson Books, 2025), 10–11.
7. Staton, *The Familiar Stranger*, 16–17.
8. Staton, *The Familiar Stranger*, 17–18.
9. Curt Thompson, *Anatomy of the Soul: Surprising Connections Between Neuroscience and Spiritual Practices That Can Transform Your Life and Relationships* (Tyndale Refresh, 2010), 16.
10. Staton, *The Familiar Stranger*, 18.
11. Staton, *The Familiar Stranger*, 18–19.
12. Staton, *The Familiar Stranger*, 103–104.
13. A. W. Tozer, *The Knowledge of the Holy* (HarperOne, 2009).
14. Staton, *The Familiar Stranger*, 29–30.
15. Staton, *The Familiar Stranger*, 30.
16. Staton, *The Familiar Stranger*, 56.
17. Staton, *The Familiar Stranger*, 59.
18. Ed D. Pytches, "Remembering John Wimber," Vineyard USA, accessed June 24, 2024, https://vineyardusa.org/remembering-john-wimber.
19. Staton, *The Familiar Stranger*, 90–91.
20. Staton, *The Familiar Stranger*, 92–93.
21. Thomas H. Green S.J., *Weeds Among the Wheat: Discernment—Where Prayer and Action Meet* (Ave Maria Press, 1984).
22. Pete Greig, *How to Hear God: A Simple Guide for Normal People* (Zondervan, 2022), 150.
23. Staton, *The Familiar Stranger*, 104–106.
24. Staton, *The Familiar Stranger*, 104.
25. Jared Patrick Boyd, *Finding Freedom in Constraint: Reimagining Spiritual Disciplines as a Communal Way of Life* (IVP, 2023), 229.
26. Staton, *The Familiar Stranger*, 108.
27. Staton, *The Familiar Stranger*, 109.
28. Dr. J. Robert Clinton, *The Making of a Leader: Recognizing the Lessons and Stages of Leadership Development*, 2nd ed. (NavPress, 2012), quoted in Staton, *Familiar Stranger*, 110–112.
29. Staton, *The Familiar Stranger*, 112.

30. David Fritch, *Enthroned: Bringing God's Kingdom to Earth Through Unceasing Worship and Prayer* (self-published, 2017), 94.

31. Dallas Willard, *Hearing God: Developing a Conversational Relationship with God* (IVP, 2012), Kindle location 995.

32. Greig, *How to Hear God*, 114.

33. Staton, *The Familiar Stranger*, 124.

34. Staton, *The Familiar Stranger*, 131.

35. Green, *Weeds Among the Wheat*, 21.

36. Staton, *The Familiar Stranger*, 121–122.

37. Staton, *The Familiar Stranger*, 131–132.

38. Greig, *How to Hear God*, 114.

39. Greig, *How to Hear God*, 114.

40. Staton, *The Familiar Stranger*, 123–124.

41. Staton, *The Familiar Stranger*, 124–126.

42. John Wimber, *Kingdom Come: Understanding What the Bible Says* (Anaheim: Vineyard Ministries International, 1988), 8.

43. Staton, *The Familiar Stranger*, 137.

44. Staton, *The Familiar Stranger*, 138.

45. Staton, *The Familiar Stranger*, 134–135.

46. Staton, *The Familiar Stranger*, 140–141.

47. Staton, *The Familiar Stranger*, 150.

48. Staton, *The Familiar Stranger*, 152–153.

49. Harold S. Kushner, *When Bad Things Happen to Good People* (Anchor, 2004), 117.

50. Staton, *The Familiar Stranger*, 175.

51. Staton, *The Familiar Stranger*, 175.

52. For a fuller explanation, see Ronald Rolheiser, *The Passion and the Cross* (Franciscan Media, 2015), 1–2.

53. Staton, *The Familiar Stranger*, 181.

54. Staton, *The Familiar Stranger*, 177.

55. Staton, *The Familiar Stranger*, 179.

56. Staton, *The Familiar Stranger*, 185–186.

ABOUT
TYLER STATON

Tyler Staton is the Lead Pastor of Bridgetown Church in Portland, Oregon, and the National Director of 24-7 Prayer USA. He is passionate about pursuing prayer—communion and conversation with God—while living deeply, poetically, wildly, and freely in the honest and gritty realities of day-to-day life. Tyler believes that justice is kinship, stories are a gift, and prayer is an invitation. He is the author of *Praying Like Monks, Living Like Fools*; *Searching for Enough: The High-Wire Walk Between Doubt and Faith*; and is the host of the *Praying Like Monks, Living Like Fools Podcast*. He lives in Portland with his wife, Kirsten, and their sons, Hank, Simon, and Amos.

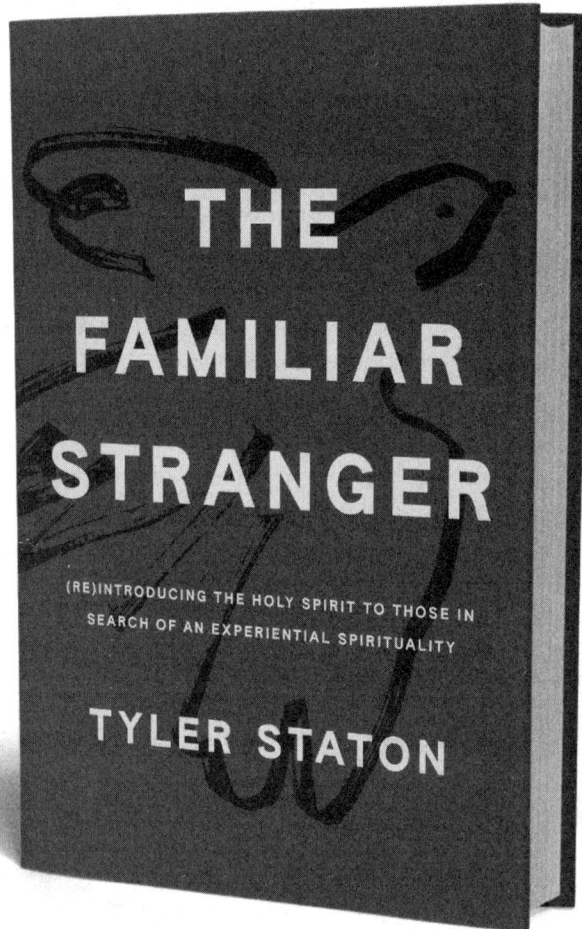